4/05

Praise for *Winning Habits*

"In *Winning Ways* Dick Lyles showed us how to work well with people. Now in *Winning Habits* he gives us the secrets to a lifetime of fulfillment."

—Spencer Johnson, author, *Who Moved My Cheese?*

"Dick Lyles brings a wealth of corporate experience and business savvy to his latest innovation, *Winning Habits*. Uniquely written through the eyes of fiction, this book does far more than entertain—it inductively teaches many profound and practical principles embodied in habits."

—Dr. Stephen R. Covey, best-selling author,
Seven Habits of Highly Effective People

"Dick Lyles has done it again. In *Winning Habits* he has given us a simple but powerful message that can make us more effective not only at work but also in our personal lives. Read it and start winning more."

—Ken Blanchard, co-author, *The One Minute Manager*®

"The quickest way to create a winning culture in your company is to have everyone read *Winning Habits* and adopt its secrets."

—Harry Paul, co-author, *Fish! A Remarkable Way
to Boost Morale and Improve Results*

"*Winning Habits* proves that Dick Lyles is becoming one of the leading parable writers of our time. This is a charming story that is sure to make a difference in your life."

—Drea Zigarmi, co-author, *Developing Leadership and Character* and Founding Partner of The Ken Blanchard Companies®

"Sustained high performance is often its own reward. *Winning Habits* can help everyone set their personal course toward lifelong fulfillment."

—Bob Nelson, Ph.D., author, *1001 Rewards @ Recognition Fieldbook* and *1001 Ways to Reward Employees*

"Everywhere we turn we hear how important it is to develop a strong work ethic. No one has ever showed us how as clearly as Dick Lyles illustrates in *Winning Habits*. This is a must read for anyone who wants to come out on top."

—Paul Stauffer, CEO, Stauffer's of Kissel Hill

WINNING HABITS

4 Secrets that Will Change
the Rest of Your Life

Dick Lyles

PEARSON
Prentice
Hall

An Imprint of PEARSON EDUCATION
Upper Saddle River, NJ • New York • London • San Francisco • Toronto • Sydney
Tokyo • Singapore • Hong Kong • Cape Town • Madrid
Paris • Milan • Munich • Amsterdam

www.ft-ph.com

A CIP record of this book can be obtained from the Library of Congress.

Production Supervisor: *Faye Gemmellaro*
Manufacturing Buyer: *Maura Zaldivar*
Cover Design Director: *Jerry Votta*
Interior Design: *Gail Cocker-Bogusz*
VP, Editor-in-Chief: *Tim Moore*
Editorial Assistant: *Richard Winkler*
Marketing Manager: *John Pierce*

 © 2004 Pearson Education, Inc.
Publishing as Prentice Hall
Upper Saddle River, New Jersey 07458

Prentice Hall offers excellent discounts on this book when ordered in quantity for bulk purchases or special sales. For more information, please contact: U.S. Corporate and Government Sales, 1-800-382-3419, corpsales@pearsontechgroup.com. For sales outside of the United States, please contact: International Sales, 1-317-581-3793, international@pearsontechgroup.com.

Company and product names mentioned herein are the trademarks or registered trademarks of their respective owners.

Printed in the United States of America

Fourth Printing

ISBN 0-13-145358-0

Pearson Education Ltd.
Pearson Education Australia Pty., Limited
Pearson Education Singapore, Pte. Ltd.
Pearson Education North Asia Ltd.
Pearson Education Canada, Ltd.
Pearson Educación de Mexico, S.A. de C.V.
Pearson Education—Japan
Pearson Education Malaysia, Pte. Ltd.

There are two kinds of people: those who help others and those who don't.

This book is dedicated to the helpers in this world—those people who consistently find ways to help others in need. May their behavior be contagious so together we can raise the standard of human existence.

Acknowledgments

Thanks first to my wife, Martha, for three-and-a-half decades of support, encouragement, and love. Her critical eye and suggestions contributed significantly to this work. Thanks also to the rest of my family, whose love and support means a great deal.

I'd like to thank Susan Fowler, Drea Zigarmi, and Marsha Wilson for their support and our continued professional relationship, which contributes a great deal to my motivation while enhancing the quality of all my efforts.

Acknowledgment is also due to Sheldon Bowles, Spencer Johnson, and Ken Blanchard for their continued support and friendship, and to Steve Piersanti for his editorial suggestions.

Special thanks goes to Ed Knappman, my literary agent, and the team at New England Publishing, and to Tim Moore—a super editor and publisher and a great guy to work with—and his team at Financial Times Prentice Hall for all they did in bringing this book to market.

WINNING HABITS

4 Secrets that Will Change
the Rest of Your Life

Winning Habits

Albert and Jennifer have lived in the Carmel Mountain Ranch area of San Diego for almost a year now. The move to California from Chicago had meant a major life change because both of them had been born and raised in the Midwest.

The move happened fairly suddenly when their employer in Chicago acquired a San Diego company that had recently become a key competitor. Right after the acquisition was announced, Jennifer was offered a promotion that involved integrating one of the new company's product lines with one that she had helped pioneer in Chicago.

To make it easy, top management had also found a job for Albert in San Diego so that they could move there together. Although Albert's job wasn't a promotion, it was at least in an area that fit nicely with his interests and talents.

At first the thought of moving so far from home was scary. They worried about being so far from friends and family and how different everything would be from what they grew up with.

But once they moved they quickly adapted to the lifestyle and the excitement of living in the Golden State. Friends and family visited them often, and the couple settled comfortably into their new jobs.

Winning Habits

Both Jennifer and Albert were more physically fit than ever going into the month of March. The southern California climate had allowed them to maintain their exercise regimen throughout the mild winter—something they always struggled with in the harsher winter months they had learned to endure in the Windy City.

They also felt more emotionally and psychologically healthy. The new chapter that had opened in their lives seemed almost like a dream come true. Even though neither could remember having dreamed this dream before, it seemed to them like they were living their dream—until Albert's nightmares began.

Albert rolled over for at least the twentieth time. He opened his weary eyes to read the glowing red numbers on the liquid crystal display of his clock radio. Four forty-three A.M. It was early Saturday morning. An hour and a half had passed since he had awakened—escaped, actually—from the horrid nightmare that caused him to break out in a cold sweat with his heart pounding like an out-of-control jackhammer. He did manage to catch himself just as he was about to let out a bloodcurdling cry for help, but not before he forced himself into a sitting position and threw the blankets aside as though they would have suffocated him had he allowed them to cover him for even another second.

Winning Habits

He sat motionless on the edge of the bed for almost five minutes as he gradually reentered the reality that surrounded him and restored his pulse and breathing to normal.

Everything and everyone were at peace in the pitch-black stillness of the midsummer morning that surrounded him. Even Digger, his pet Australian shepherd, who had been barking up a fit half an hour earlier at some stray cat, was peacefully curled up and soundly sleeping in his favorite corner of the patio.

Peace and calm permeated everything. Everything, that was, except Albert, who was anything but serene.

Geez, I can't believe I didn't wake Jennifer up, he thought. *That was almost exactly the same dream I had three nights ago. Maybe if I just sit here and think myself back through the dream, I can get rid of these feelings so they don't stay with me all day like they did last time.*

So as best he could, he recalled the images, even though the sequence often didn't make sense. It started like a normal, any-night dream. He saw himself going to work. Everyone he passed on his walk from the parking lot to his office was polite and friendly, even though there wasn't a familiar face in the crowd. They were all strangers. He noticed himself casually reflecting about how young everyone looked, but he didn't think it was any big deal.

Winning Habits

Then he arrived at his office, with all its familiar trappings, and he felt comfortable and at home. After flipping his computer on and checking his voice mail messages, he picked up an envelope from the center of his desk. It was his paycheck from his employer, United Global Applied Technologies (UGAT). The first thing he noticed as he looked it over was that his gross pay was one dollar and ninety-eight cents! After deductions this left him with a net take home pay of one dollar and seventeen cents. Then he noticed the date. It was for twenty years in the future!

As he arose from his chair to take the check to the payroll department, he found himself trapped in a cage that was floating somewhere in the basement of UGAT. But even though it was a cage, he couldn't grab hold of the bars. Something kept him contained, and he couldn't figure out what it was. Outside the cage was a constant parade of people he worked with at UGAT. They were on different escalators that had the characteristics of never-ending magic carpets. These wavy escalators surrounded his cell and caused all the people to float like magic into the distant upper reaches of the building. As they floated on their upward journey, they laughed and joked and carried on. It was like they were going to some big party in the sky where there would be gifts galore for all.

All the people were oblivious to Albert. He was invisible to them. He tried to claw at the cell and free himself, but he couldn't make contact. He repeatedly tried to cry out to them, but no sound came from his mouth. He desperately wanted to join up, to be part of all the excitement, but he was completely constrained by unseen forces. It was when he had reached deep down inside to scream at them with all his might that he had suddenly awakened in his panic-stricken sweat.

Now, even though he turned off the vision, the feelings continued to saturate his entire being.

Finally he lay back down and rearranged the blankets. But try as he might, he couldn't get back to sleep. He knew what had caused the dream, and it made him miserable. So he tossed and turned and talked to himself. Only it wasn't much of a conversation. It was mostly just questions he kept asking but couldn't answer.

What am I doing wrong? **he would ask himself over and over again.** *Am I obsolete? Worthless? At the end of my career already?* **Panic overtook him again and caused a knot to form tightly in his stomach.**

I'm not even thirty years old yet, **he reflected,** *and everybody I know is going places except me.*

First it was Megan. When she had been promoted a year ago, it caught Albert by surprise. She had been his first supervisor, and it never occurred to him that he would ever work for anyone else. But after thinking it through a bit, he realized it was only natural that she would move up. After all, she had the talent and was already in management anyway.

Then came Jennifer's promotion, which had prompted their move to San Diego. Even though Albert got a new job when they transferred, he stayed at the same salary and grade level. Because they were both excited about the move, he didn't think much about it at the time.

Then five weeks ago Chip and Elizabeth got tapped for higher-level jobs. Albert had been close to both and liked them a lot. He had worked with the two for most of the past year on the Maritime Industries project, during which time the three had developed a special bond. *Now they're off doing even more challenging projects,* thought Albert, *and here I am doing the cleanup work for Maritime.*

Then two weeks ago when Whitney and Alison got promoted out of Albert's department, the emotions—and the self-doubt—began to reach tidal wave proportions.

With all these new people around me, he thought, *I feel like an old shoe, getting nudged slowly but surely into the most isolated corner of the closet.*

"It's about time you got some sleep," Jennifer grumbled as Albert fitfully rolled over yet again. "Are you ever going to tell me what's wrong?"

Winning Habits

Albert ignored her.

Why won't he talk to me about it? she asked herself as she tried to get back to sleep.

Jennifer had first realized that something was bugging Albert a week earlier when he completely forgot their fifth wedding anniversary. He had never done anything like that before.

I have to be careful about how I bring this up, he thought. Not now, though. Maybe when we take Digger for his walk in the park. No, too many distractions. I want to talk about this. Maybe over breakfast. Yeah, that'd be good. Then if it leads to a deeper discussion, we can just stay right there until we finish.

I'll be careful how I say it, so she doesn't think this is about her, Albert thought as he recalled the promotion Jennifer had received when they moved.

Albert reflected on the promotion again. She clearly deserved the promotion and it was the right decision for the company. It wasn't until after the move that he had even thought about promotion for himself, mostly because he liked his work and had developed a genuine affection for the people he worked with. But after they had settled somewhat, for the first time in his life he started to think about climbing up the career ladder.

He often wondered what promotional opportunities might someday come his way, even though he didn't do anything to pursue advancement.

Now it had become almost an obsession. Four close friends had been promoted during the past month, and it appeared as though he wasn't even being considered.

What's wrong with me? Albert asked himself for the ten thousandth time as he rolled over yet again.

Why am I not happy? he continued. Jennifer and I have enjoyed a great relationship for six years. We both like San Diego, we both like the company we work for, we both like the work we do, and we love Digger. Why do I feel so empty? Unwanted?

On two different occasions during the past few months, he had asked his new boss why no promotional opportunities had come his way.

"No real reason," his boss had answered. "Just hang in there."

Great, thought Albert. *What kind of an answer is that?*

He longed for the "good old days" when Megan had been his boss. She always seemed to have a reasonable answer for questions like this. But she had been promoted long ago, and now that he was in another division, he didn't want to impose.

So here he was. Powerless. Lost. Alone.

Winning Habits

The sun rose to welcome a beautiful Saturday morning that was every bit as peaceful as the night had been for everyone except Albert. He pulled his pillow over his head to isolate himself from the new day.

Jennifer awakened slightly and snuggled close to Albert, her thoughts focused only on him. She wanted desperately to talk to him about "it," whatever "it" was. She was frustrated because she couldn't come up with an obvious answer.

But she knew whatever it was, it was troubling him deeply. Although missing their anniversary was what caused her to realize something was wrong, there had been other events. *Like when he ran out of gas on his way to work,* she thought. *Or even worse was the time he forgot to flip the locking latch on the lavatory door on the flight to Atlanta.* An elderly lady wanting to use the lavatory had opened the door and literally caught Albert with his pants down. *Who could ever do something like that?* she wondered.

Albert simply continued along in his somnambulistic state; half asleep, half awake, fretfully trying to sort out his situation.

Jennifer spoke first. "Not much sleep again, huh?"

Albert didn't say anything.

"Okay, then. Come on. Let's take Digger to the park."

Winning Habits

"Uh uh," mumbled Albert, pulling the pillow back over his head. Even though he planned to have his talk with Jennifer, he didn't want to get out of bed.

"Come on," she said, tugging at the pillow. "Look what a great day it is."

"Just another fifteen minutes," he begged.

"Oh, all right," she responded as she got up and went into the kitchen to put on some coffee. Then she let Digger out to retrieve the morning newspaper.

In fifteen minutes she returned to the bedroom, bounced onto the bed, pulled the covers off Albert, and said, "Your fifteen minutes are up. Let's go." She bounced up and down in a kneeling position beside Albert in an effort to get his energy flowing. "Come on, Albert."

"Another fifteen minutes," he begged.

"No," Jennifer responded as she continued to bounce. "You had your fifteen minutes."

Then she paused. "Maybe you're catching something"

"I'm just tired. Sorry."

"There are some weird bugs going around."

"Nah, I'm just tired."

Winning Habits

"Want to talk about it?" she asked.

"I'm just tired."

"Albert, what's wrong? Is it me?"

"No, it's not you. Just fifteen minutes more."

"You already had fifteen minutes. Let's go. Digger's waiting."

"Stop bouncing," he complained. "I need more sleep."

"Oh, to heck with you," she said. "Sleep all you want. We'll go without you."

Finally he decided it was time to get it done. "No," he said. "Let's just go to the French Cafe and get some breakfast. We'll take Digger later."

"Okay," she said. "Anything's better than lying around here all day. But let's get going now."

Maybe my good news will cheer him up, she thought. She had wanted to tell him during their walk in the park. *Now I'll just tell him at breakfast.* She was so excited about it, she was sure some of her excitement would have to rub off on Albert. *Maybe it'll get him out of it and back to normal.*

Albert pulled himself out of bed.

"About time," declared Jennifer. "Hurry up. Let's go to the French Cafe. I'm starved, and I've got some good news."

Winning Habits

"I'm coming," replied Albert.

The best way to handle this is to play it straight, thought Albert. *I'll just tell her I don't want her to worry about anything—that I need to work this through myself. Then I'll tell her plain and simple that I've been thinking a lot about the possibility of moving up, but I haven't quite figured out how to make it happen. She'll want to jump in and help, but I'll just tell her I need to work things through for myself.*

Meantime, Jennifer was in a quandary. *Geez, this is frustrating,* she thought. *I hope he gets in touch with himself sometime soon. Oh well, whatever it is, if it isn't about me, at least my good news ought to cheer him up for a while.*

Luckily, their favorite table on the front patio opened up just as they arrived at the French Cafe. They loved sitting outdoors for breakfast on Saturday mornings, something they never did in Chicago.

The waitress quickly poured them fresh coffee and they both ordered eggs Florentine and one of the light cinnamon buns they could share. They carried out their ritual of dividing up the morning paper and began scanning through it while waiting for their food. Although Albert leafed through the sports section, he wasn't paying much attention. He was too busy mustering up the courage and trying to find the right words to share his concerns with Jennifer.

Their food came, and they put the newspaper aside.

Now, thought Jennifer. *This is a great time to cheer him up.*

"Guess what, Albert?"

"Uh, what?" responded Albert as he raised a big forkful of eggs and spinach to his mouth.

"I'm so excited," she said. "Yesterday afternoon the head of the new Industrial Services Division called me in to his office and offered me a position with his group. It's a fabulous promotion!"

To say Albert was stunned would be a gross understatement. Flabbergasted might be a better word. He almost coughed out his mouthful of food. His throat tightened so much he couldn't swallow. He couldn't even chew. He just sat there, struggling to regain control as Jennifer continued.

"Isn't that great, Albert? Of course we should talk it over before I decide to take it, but it sounds like an incredible opportunity. What do you think? He said he's already talked to my boss, and we could complete the transition in about a month."

Albert finally managed to regain some jaw movement and massage the eggy mass that now threatened to suffocate him. His mind similarly began to massage the new information from Jennifer.

Winning Habits

"I think the timing is just about perfect for me. And that division has just landed several great new projects with some really neat challenges. Isn't this great news, Albert?"

Somehow he was able to swallow a small portion of the eggs Florentine, freeing himself to emit a feeble, monosyllabic response. "Great," he said, slowly nodding his head up and down. The blob of food that remained in his mouth now felt like a chunk of clay seeking to completely stifle his conversation.

Fortunately, Jennifer's enthusiasm carried the moment. As she excitedly shared with Albert all her thoughts about this great new opportunity, he mostly listened and occasionally asked questions.

Raising his problem now was completely out of the question. No way could he discuss his own lack of promotion with Jennifer under these circumstances. It might cause her to feel guilty about her own success. *That's the last thing I want,* thought Albert. *I don't want my shortcomings to be a burden for her.* It pleased him to see her so happy, and he didn't want to spoil it.

She continued to talk about it all the way home.

When they arrived home, Jennifer hustled off to call a few friends while Albert went into the backyard to toss the Frisbee with Digger. However, he soon lost interest because his heart wasn't in it.

Winning Habits

Albert walked around to the front of the house and began idly pulling weeds from the flowerbeds lining the yard. He hadn't noticed that Mrs. O'Reilly, his next-door neighbor, had been tending her yard, too. He noticed her garden cart and tools in the driveway just as she ambled out of her garage with a tray of purple pansies ready for planting.

"Good afternoon, Albert," she chimed. "Great day for yard work, isn't it?"

"Oh. Hi, Mrs. O'Reilly. Yeah, I guess so," Albert replied feebly.

Albert guessed she was in her mid-seventies. But she was one of those people who, after turning sixty, didn't seem to age. She could have been in her eighties for all he knew. But one thing was certain. She loved people, she loved life, and she loved the world around her. She brought cheer and pleasantness wherever she went.

"Stauffers had a sale on these pansies so I thought I'd add a little color to the yard."

"Great idea. They'll look really neat."

"You don't seem too cheery given the splendor of this day, Albert."

Mrs. O'Reilly's penetrating candor always intrigued Albert. But it was one of the things he liked about her. She was direct without being rude, and she possessed a great deal more sensitivity to what people were thinking and feeling than anyone he had ever known. If anyone had a sixth sense about people, it was Mrs. O'Reilly. But her manner always ensured that any conversation with her would take place on a deeper and more meaningful plane than a similar conversation with anyone else.

"It is a nice day, isn't it?" responded Albert.

"The day's a great one, Albert," she said as she looked up from her tray of pansies with a twinkle in her eye. "It's you I'm not so sure about."

He knew she had him pegged. He could either find some excuse to walk away right now or get into it with her. She had always had great insights and he knew from past experience that she would do no harm to anyone under any circumstances. Since he couldn't talk about it with Jennifer, why not Mrs. O'Reilly?

"May I ask you something?"

"Any time, Albert," she replied with a wink.

"Just between you and me? I mean it's not about Jennifer, but I don't know if I want her to know about this just yet."

"You'll tell her when the time's right, I'm sure," she responded with her characteristic twinkle.

Winning Habits

So Albert told her the whole story. Getting it off his chest made him feel better.

She listened to every detail, which didn't take much time to recount. When he was finished, she responded.

"The first thing you need to realize, Albert, is that you're not alone. I know that doesn't help much when you're the one who's suffering. But it means that others have gone through this successfully and you can, too."

"I never thought of that," said Albert.

"It's hard to think of the struggles other people have endured when you're caught up in your own. But it's true."

"Can you help me, then?" asked Albert.

"I can't. But I know who can."

"You do?"

"Certainly. He's the best, and if you bring me that big bag of fertilizer over there, it won't cost you a cent to learn more."

Albert quickly hauled the bag to where she had planted her pansies. Just the thought of help being out there somewhere caused Albert to start to feel better.

"Who is it?" he asked.

"My brother-in-law. Admiral John P. J. Farragut."

Winning Habits

"Admiral Farragut? *The* Admiral Farragut? He's your brother-in-law?" asked Albert incredulously.

"Has been for nearly half a century."

"Wow," exclaimed Albert, still processing this newly acquired bit of information while reviewing in his mind what he knew about Admiral John P. J. Farragut.

The man was a national hero. His middle initials stood for Paul Jones, so his full name was John Paul Jones Farragut—*Admiral John Paul Jones Farragut*. He was named after the father of the American Navy, John Paul Jones. The "Farragut" part of his name implied he was a direct descendant of another American naval hero, Admiral David Glasgow Farragut, which he was. It was this Admiral Farragut who, during the Civil War, in Mobile Bay, said, "Damn the torpedoes—full steam ahead!"

Not only did John Paul Jones Farragut inherit Admiral David Glasgow Farragut's genes, but his parents had also raised him in an environment teeming with special expectations. Even before he was born, his parents decided that it was time for the Farragut lineage to produce another icon in the annals of the U.S. Navy.

His popularity among his peers took root during his years at the Naval Academy. John Paul Jones Farragut had been a popular midshipman because of his winning ways. People liked to be around him in large part because he built people up. He always seemed to make people feel stronger as a result of their interactions with him. He also found ways to cause everyone's priorities to mesh, so people pulled together better when John was around. And when those around him polarized around a particular issue, John was always the one to loosen people up and lead them to a shared perspective.

The final trait that gave him a special way with people was his knack for solving problems by looking forward rather than backward. While everyone else tended to try to fix the blame, John always focused on producing a better result in the future.

As a commander of one of the famed riverboat squadrons, his exploits and "damn the torpedoes" attitude became legendary.

Subsequently, he became only the second admiral in history to command first the Atlantic Fleet, then the Pacific. After that he became Chief of Naval Operations and then Chairman of the Joint Chiefs of Staff.

In retirement he served on the Boards of Directors of several of the world's most prestigious corporations. But he gained even more recognition for his work with nonprofit children's organizations.

He had become a legend in his own time. High schools, streets, and even a stadium had been named after him.

Winning Habits

"Wow!" exclaimed Albert coming back from his reverie.

"If you'd like, I can see if the Admiral would meet with you," offered Mrs. O'Reilly. "He usually spends Sundays on that yacht of his, so if you're interested in driving over to Coronado, he might even be able to see you tomorrow."

"That'd be unbelievable," said Albert. "Jennifer has plans to meet some old college friends who are in town for a convention, so it would work great for me."

Still in awe, Albert asked, "He's really your brother-in-law?"

"Certainly is," beamed Mrs. O'Reilly.

Sunday afternoon came quickly. The Admiral agreed to meet on his sailing yacht, which was moored at a marina on Coronado Island. Albert showed up at the marina exactly at the appointed hour of one o'clock.

The Admiral's yacht wasn't hard to locate. It was moored at the end of the longest pier in the marina. Although it wasn't the largest, it was by far the most remarkable. Everything about it shone in the glistening sunshine. It was immaculate, its beauty overpowering the other vessels moored nearby.

Albert hesitated on the pier alongside the yacht. He wasn't sure whether it was because he was afraid that he might somehow spoil the magnificence of this masterpiece by walking on it, or whether he was intimidated by the prospect of meeting Admiral John Paul Jones Farragut. As it turned out neither fear mattered, because in a mere instant the icon made his appearance, popping halfway out of the boat's cabin and slapping an arm over the rail, sizing up Albert with a piercing gaze.

Albert was mesmerized. The Admiral's hair was thick, silver-gray, and wavy. His eyebrows were equally as gray, and were also thick and bushy, but they looked as though they had been recently charged with static electricity, causing the hairs to stand out almost an inch from either side of his forehead. His blue eyes, deep set against the silver brows, were intriguing. One could almost conjure up images of Kris Kringle if the eyes only were taken into account.

But beneath them was a face carved of marble, set on a squared jaw that projected authority more than affection. It was easy to see how the Admiral had assumed command in so many different situations. He exuded a commanding presence from every pore of his body.

"You must be Albert."

"Yes, sir," replied Albert. He couldn't remember ever calling anyone "sir" before, but it seemed the only natural thing to say at the moment.

"Come aboard. Mrs. O'Reilly thinks highly of you."

"Thank you," responded Albert as he stepped over the gunwales and into the cockpit of the yacht.

Winning Habits

"And your wife, Jennifer. Mrs. O'Reilly talks about her a lot."

"Thanks," responded Albert. "I think she's neat, too."

"Sounds like you're real happy together."

"We've got a great relationship."

"I'm sure you do," said the Admiral, as he climbed out of the cabin and sat on one side of the cockpit while he gestured to Albert to sit on the other.

"Mrs. O'Reilly's a great neighbor," said Albert, trying to broaden the focus of the conversation a bit.

"And a great lady," added the Admiral. "She tells me you're feeling stuck in your career at the moment."

"Yes, sir," confirmed Albert.

"Tell me about it."

So Albert did. Periodically the Admiral asked clarifying questions, but for the most part he just listened as Albert recounted his work history at UGAT and told the Admiral what his job had been like.

When Albert was finished, they both sat in silence as the Admiral reflected on everything he had heard.

After a few eternal moments, the Admiral finally broke the silence. "It sounds to me like you need to examine some of your habits, young man."

23

Winning Habits

"Habits?" asked Albert. After all, he didn't smoke, he drank only occasionally, and he had stopped biting his fingernails when he was in high school.

"Habits," declared the Admiral.

"Okay," responded Albert hesitantly. He had no idea where this conversation was headed.

"When I said 'habits,' you probably thought of all kinds of negative stuff, and things that people ought to stop doing."

"Yes, sir, I guess I did," recalled Albert. *Did he read my mind?*

"Well, habits can be good things, too. One thing they don't do enough of these days is teach people good habits."

Albert tried to think of a time when anyone, including all his teachers, had actually tried to teach him a habit. He couldn't come up with anything.

"A few good habits will carry you a long way," said the Admiral. "They'll get you through some tough times and set you up for consistent success. They'll make you a pacesetter."

"A pacesetter?" asked Albert. He was genuinely interested in what the Admiral had to say.

"A pacesetter," declared the Admiral as he looked deep into Albert's eyes to drive the point home. He made sure he was getting through to Albert completely before he continued.

"People talk a lot about leaders and leadership, and most of it's worthwhile. Study leadership and learn about leading, and it'll do you a lot of good. But I think learning to be a pacesetter is even more important. This more than anything else will determine whether or not you triumph in your career."

Again he paused without blinking or breaking eye contact. It was as though he were looking straight into Albert's mind as he talked. The Admiral meant business and wasn't about to risk being misunderstood. Likewise, Albert didn't dare break the trancelike connection he felt with the Admiral.

"Sometimes you're in a position to lead and sometimes you're not. But you're always in a position to be a pacesetter."

The Admiral paused for a moment before continuing.

"When you are handed the reins of leadership, you want to take them and do well. But I'll give it to you straight. You need to make good things happen around you *whether or not you're the leader.* Do that consistently and any position of responsibility you want will be offered sooner than you can imagine."

Albert didn't say a word because he didn't want to soften the Admiral's intensity. He also wanted to find out what this all meant.

"Don't seek career advancement by looking for promotions. Seek the opportunity to make good things happen around you, and the rewards will follow."

Winning Habits

"But I've always done good work," countered Albert. "That doesn't seem to be my problem."

"And you're smart, too," observed the Admiral.

"Then I'm stumped," proclaimed Albert. "Which is it? My work isn't good enough? Or I'm not smart enough?"

"I'm sure your work is good enough, and I can tell you're smart enough. But you need to make more good things happen around you—that's the booster you need."

"I still don't get it," said Albert.

"Of course not. If you did, you wouldn't be here with me," laughed the Admiral, lifting his famous chin skyward. "But because you are here, I'm going to share four secrets that will change your life by jump-starting your stalled career. But first let's get underway."

To Albert's surprise, they set sail out of the marina and into San Diego Harbor with the Coronado Bay Bridge looming majestically overhead. After a few moments at the helm, with the course set, the Admiral turned his piercing glare back toward Albert.

"You say you do good work," observed the Admiral.

"I'm not the only one. Others say it, too. I get a lot of compliments and my fair share of recognition."

Winning Habits

"More than or less than what they say about your peers at UGAT?"

"There are a lot of good people at UGAT. Most of them do good work that's fairly recognized," explained Albert.

"Hah!" exclaimed the Admiral.

Albert waited for him to say more, but he just stood behind the wheel of the yacht, looking away from Albert, out over the water ahead, and wearing a quirky smile. Finally he turned his gaze back to Albert.

"Don't you see?" he asked Albert.

"I guess not," came the response.

"You *all* do good work." The Admiral was pleased with his explanation, even though Albert was perplexed.

After a moment, the Admiral spoke again. "You need to be different in a way that doesn't detract from their efforts, but allows you to make an even greater contribution."

"How do I do that?" asked Albert.

"I'm going to share the four secrets. The first one I learned as a high school baseball player. Our school had a good team with a lot of good players. Our coach always told us the reason he worked us so hard every day was so we could play at the college level. But at the same time he said if we were to succeed at that level—or for that matter in anything that is important in life—we should make a habit of doing more than what's required.

Almost automatically, Albert raised his eyebrows and nodded his head to one side.

"Skeptical?" asked the Admiral.

"I've heard that before," responded Albert. "I don't mean to be disrespectful or anything, but it seems to me to be one of those motivational kind of things that sounds great when you say it, but doesn't make sense when you think about actually doing it."

"Explain," said the Admiral.

"Well, since you brought up baseball, let's use that. Say you're on base. If you cross home safely, you score one run. You can't back up and cross home twice on the same play to score two runs. Nor can you run past home plate and all the way to the dugout and score a run and a half. In other words, if you do what's required, you score one run. If you don't, you don't. It's simple, the rules are clear, and there isn't any extra effort that will change them."

"Aha!" responded the Admiral. "But the extra effort very rarely comes at the time of the play—the moment of truth, if you will. More often than not, the extra effort comes before the moment of truth so

you'll be optimally prepared when the test comes. For example, one of the things that coach taught us was always to be 'first on and last off.' "

" 'First on and last off'?" questioned Albert.

" 'First on and last off' means you put in more effort and work harder than anyone else—and not just busy work, but a meaningful, higher level of contribution. Get to work—or meetings, presentations, problem-solving sessions—early, and don't be the first to leave. Those times, early and late, are often when some of the most meaningful contributions are made. When we played baseball it meant being the first one to show up for practice and the last to go home. It meant doing more to prepare and develop than our competition. It meant putting in more meaningful effort to produce the end result."

Albert thought about this. It intrigued him that some of life's important lessons could be learned from the world of sports.

"Do you like baseball?" asked the Admiral.

"I don't play, but I love to go to the games."

"Who is San Diego's most famous, and most successful, baseball player ever?"

"That's easy: Tony Gwynn," answered Albert.

Winning Habits

"What made him so great?" asked the Admiral.

"That's easy, too," answered Albert. "He's most known for his eight national league batting titles, but he was also a great fielder. In addition to all his batting titles, he also won five Golden Glove Awards for his play in the outfield."

"Hah!" exclaimed the Admiral. "Wrong answer!"

Albert waited for the Admiral to continue, but he didn't. Instead he just stared out over the water, shaking his head back and forth, as the sailboat sliced through the water. Finally Albert broke the silence.

"I don't get it."

"Maybe you got the wrong answer because you answered the wrong question," the Admiral responded.

Albert thought about that for a while. Then he said, "I still don't get it."

"I asked you why he was so great, and you told me why he was so famous," the Admiral explained with a chuckle. "He was famous because he was a great performer both at the plate and in the outfield. He was a great performer because he was always first on and last off!"

"I remember reading about that," said Albert.

"Even after twenty years and winning all those awards, he still showed up early, took extra swings—more than any of his teammates—and often stayed after the games were over so he could get even more work in. He studied videotapes of his batting efforts so he could correct any flaws before the next game. He was *great* because he always put in the extra effort to prepare for his moment of truth."

"And it obviously paid off," observed Albert.

"Indeed it did. But it only paid off for him because it became part of him. You see, habits are more than merely devices or behavioral gimmicks you employ once in a while. True habits become defining elements of your character."

"Something you do all the time," observed Albert.

"It goes even deeper than that," explained the Admiral. "They're ingrained behavior patterns that become such an integral part of you that if you didn't do them you'd be miserable."

"Look at Tony Gwynn some more," the Admiral continued. "When he retired as a player, but before he started coaching at San Diego State, he worked as a baseball commentator for ESPN. After his first show, he reviewed a tape of his effort. Like most people who watch themselves on tape, he was horrified. All the people around him told him not to watch himself on tape like that because it was the most con- fidence-shattering, frustrating thing a person could do. Gwynn's response was to explain that self-critiquing by studying his swing on tape had helped him to stay on top for twenty years in the big leagues. He couldn't imagine not doing the same thing as a sportscaster. Because this was a habit—a defining characteristic of himself in his mind—the discomfort that he would experience by not doing it would be substantially greater than the discomfort he experienced by watching himself."

"I watched him that year, and his improvements were noticeable," said Albert.

"At the Naval Academy, our main rival was the Military Academy at West Point. We competed against them in every sport we played, and our overriding goal was to beat Army at every opportunity. So we built that superordinate goal into everything we did. For example, during the hazing we endured our first year, an upperclassman would often make us drop and do fifty pushups. We would count out the fifty and then do one more while shouting, 'And one to beat Army!'. Everything we did, we always did the amount demanded plus one more 'to beat Army.' "

"But what does beating Army have to do with everything else in life?" asked Albert.

"That's an easy one," responded the Admiral. "Ultimately, the focus changes to whatever you're doing. It's the habit of thinking about doing an extra one that matters. After a year of always thinking about doing something extra in everything you do, it becomes habit forming, just like it did with Tony Gwynn. So later on in life whenever you're assigned a project or you commit to achieving a goal, and you complete the necessary steps, you will automatically remind yourself to go the extra mile for good measure. That one bit of extra effort will most often turn out to be what pushes you out in front or ensures that your goal will be met."

"Sounds like it's worth a try," replied Albert. He made a mental note to himself to capture the thought in his computer when he got home. This is what he pictured.

The first Winning Habit:

Be first on, last off, and add extra value!

Interesting, **Albert thought. He tried to recall what his attitude usually was when he finished most projects. Invariably, his attitude had been to let someone else worry about the details and the follow-through.**

"Tell me what you're thinking," prodded the Admiral.

"I'm thinking how different that is from the way I've always been," responded Albert.

"How so?"

"I always throw myself into a project up front. I put a lot of energy into things until the lion's share of the thinking is done. Then I start losing interest. I get eager to move on to the next big challenge. I never really thought about it before, but that does frustrate others on the project. It drives Jennifer crazy."

"She's not that way?" pursued the Admiral.

"Not at all. I've always just thought of her as being too com-pulsive—that she pays too much attention to detail."

"But it's not merely attention to detail, is it?"

"I guess not. Now that I think about it, she often comes up with significant improvements to the project long after I've moved on to something else. In fact, as I think more about it, if I wanted to really be brutal with myself, I'd have to say that extra effort on her part usually means better results, too."

"So some people who might be watching all this might conclude that you both have great ideas and do good work, but Jennifer gets better results," the Admiral offered. "And it sounds to me like Jennifer's extra effort has a different focus than you've thought it has. It's results-based rather than activity-based. Her energy goes into creating a better outcome, not merely handling more details for the sake of being more detailed."

"Wow," said Albert. "I never thought of it like that. I just always thought we both did good work in different ways.

But there's something else. She's also better at the part of the secret that says you should be first on and last off."

"Meaning?"

"She's always among the first to be anywhere and the last to leave. We even take separate cars to work because I usually show up late and don't like to hang around when it's time to go home."

"So the question becomes, if you were a higher-level manager in the organization and had to choose between you and Jennifer for a promotion, who would you choose?"

"Since I'd be more concerned about results, I'd choose Jennifer."

"Hah!" exclaimed the Admiral. "Her habits work."

Wow, thought Albert. *It does make sense, but could it make that much difference?*

Just then the Admiral spun the wheel and shouted, "Ready about! Helm's alee!" as the boat turned into the wind with a great flapping of the sails. In a short time the Admiral had settled on a new course in the general direction of the marina entrance.

After a few moments the Admiral again spoke. "Smart people—and you're one of 'em—often make a

big mistake. They think their brains alone will carry 'em. In school that's often the case. But in the real world, brains alone aren't enough."

Albert thought about this without responding.

"Even Albert Einstein agreed with this."

"Einstein?" asked Albert. *He possessed one of the best brains ever.*

"Yep. Einstein," responded the Admiral. "When he was alive, people were always asking him about his intelligence: how he got it, who he inherited it from, and the like. And all that speculation bothered him because he believed his intelligence—or raw brain power—had very little to do with his success."

"He did?"

"Sure did. Said it in a lot of different ways to a lot of different folks, but he said it most eloquently in a letter he wrote to a physician friend of his by the name of Hans Musan."

"What did he say?"

"Musan had written to Einstein, as had a lot of folks, asking him about his ancestors and who he might have inherited his genius from. Einstein responded by writing that as far as his ancestors or forebears were concerned, no one knew much about them, and if they had any special gifts or traits, they weren't obvious to anyone who knew them. Then he went on to write, and I quote,

Winning Habits

I know quite certainly that I, myself, have no special gifts. Curiosity, obsession, and dogged endurance, combined with self-critique, have brought me my ideas.

" 'Curiosity, obsession, and dogged endurance, combined with self-critique,' " repeated Albert.

"You won't find anyone who's been successful in any field who doesn't have an almost insatiable curiosity about what they do. Obsession merely means maintaining a passionate commitment. The dogged endurance is important to help you overcome all the obstacles that inevitably will stand in your way. But the one most people miss is self-critique. And it's probably the most important."

"It's not always easy to do," responded Albert.

"I agree. But you've just made a good start by evaluating yourself against the first habit. And critiquing yourself while looking at Jennifer's strengths was beneficial. Most people do just the opposite. They look at what's good about them-selves and what's weak in someone else, and then they get frustrated by asking 'Why me?' or 'Why not me?' "

"That's what I've been doing a lot of lately," observed Albert.

"So your energy has been channeled into frustration, blame, and getting depressed, rather than into making the changes you need to make."

Winning Habits

"Exactly." Albert started feeling better already.
Probably because for the first time in a long time, I'm
feeling like I know what to do to make a meaningful
change, **he thought.**

"Let's come about and head for port," said the Admiral as
he spun the wheel once again and the yacht turned its bow
toward the entrance to the marina. "I'll share the second
secret with you on the way in, and then we'll plan another
time to get together."

Albert ducked as the boom swung over the cockpit in a
flawless maneuver. In a moment they were on course and
headed toward the buoys at the entrance to the marina.

"The second secret is akin to the first," explained the Admiral.

"I'm all ears," said Albert.

"It's akin to the first, but in many ways it's much harder to
put into practice. At least it was for me."

Albert marveled that *anything* could be hard for the Admiral
to do.

"The second secret is 'Never trade results for excuses.' "

"Why is that so hard?" asked Albert. "Not to be disrespectful or anything, but it seems like everyone would want results
rather than excuses."

Winning Habits

"It's putting it into practice every day that makes it hard. It means never accepting an excuse for your performance. It means always being willing to say to yourself and to others about your own efforts that there is never an excuse that will take the place of results. You simply develop the habit of saying 'There's no excuse.' "

" 'There's no excuse'?" asked Albert.

"When I learned it, we said 'There's no excuse, sir.' But you can just say 'There's no excuse.' "

" 'There's no excuse,' " repeated Albert. "It's easy enough to say, but I don't get it."

"Sometimes it's not at all easy to say. That's why you need to practice it and make sure it becomes a habit, so when the difficult times come, you will still be comfortable saying it."

Albert felt uncomfortable. "I don't mean any disrespect, sir. But I'm not sure I follow you."

"This is another valuable secret I learned at the Academy. Although a lot of the hazing we were subjected to was ridiculous, some of it served a valuable purpose—there were important lessons to be learned. This secret was one where the lesson learned was invaluable."

Albert continued to listen.

Winning Habits

"During the hazing we were told to do a number of things. At every meal we'd sit at a table with four plebes and eight upperclassmen. The upperclassmen would fire questions at us plebes a mile a minute. Most of the questions focused on things we didn't know, but needed to learn. We could never respond by saying 'I don't know.' Nor could we guess. If we didn't know the correct answer, the only acceptable way to respond was by saying 'I'll find out, sir.' Then we were required to find out all the answers to all the questions we didn't know by the next meal, or have hell to pay. The hardest ones to find out were between breakfast and lunch and lunch and dinner, because we had to go to class, participate in sports, and do at least a dozen other things along the way. So invariably, we'd forget a question or not be able to find the answer in the time allotted. But the upperclassmen never forgot. So when they asked the question again at the next meal and we didn't know the answer, we'd say 'I'll find out, sir.' They'd respond by reminding us that that's what we'd said during the last meal, and then they'd say, 'So, why didn't you find out?' No matter how good your reasons were, you could never give an excuse. The only acceptable response was, 'There's no excuse, sir.' "

"That sounds unfair," said Albert.

"And at first it seemed that way to us," agreed the Admiral.

"What happened if you really did have an excuse?"

"We still had to answer that there was no excuse."

"But maybe there was a legitimate reason. If there was a reason, would that be an excuse?" asked Albert.

"You're saying the same thing, Albert. An excuse is nothing more than a justification or explanation for doing or not doing something. The lesson is that if you commit to something, you should do it. Your standard for letting yourself off the hook should be high—not something you let go of easily with some simple rationalization."

"But stuff happens," said Albert.

"It does," agreed the Admiral. "But people who let stuff get in the way don't reach the top. Successful people meet their commitments."

"It almost sounds too unrealistic," said Albert.

"At first it did to us, too. But once we developed the habit, that saying changed the way we thought about our commitments forever."

"How?"

"First off, it made each of us reflect on how many times we hadn't done something we said we'd do and used some flimsy excuse as an out. Second, it made us reflect on whether or not we actually could have done what we promised if we'd been more alert or managed our time better. Usually we could have."

"But there had to have been times when it was virtually impossible."

"There were. But that didn't matter. If you didn't get the job done, all the excuses in the world didn't matter. The fact was you failed to achieve what you set out to do. Excuses are never a substitute for results. Period."

"There's that focus on results again," said Albert.

"That's right, Albert. Activity does not equal productivity. It's the result that counts and you should never accept an excuse for falling short."

"It still sounds a bit brutal," observed Albert.

"Only at first," agreed the Admiral. "But once you accept the premise and make it a habit not to accept excuses, you'll find it makes things a whole lot easier. For example, how many times have you missed a deadline or failed to meet a project objective for what seemed like a good excuse, and then subsequently looked back and regretted accepting the excuse because the missed result meant too much?"

Albert reflected for a moment. "Well, when you put it that way, I can think of an example that happened just a few weeks ago."

Winning Habits

"Tell me about it," urged the Admiral.

"It was a proposal we were working on for a new customer. We knew we needed to include some examples of previous work, but the computer network was down so we couldn't access them easily. We made a note in the proposal that we would provide samples later if necessary, but we didn't include them because of the computer breakdown. We thought it was a good enough excuse. But we didn't get the contract. Our competitor—whose overall proposal wasn't as good—got the job because they provided all the required information. Afterward we felt bad because we knew that if we'd just put in a little extra effort and got the samples by bypassing the computer, we would have been successful."

"Great example!" exclaimed the Admiral. "So you can see how things would have turned out differently if you had the habit of saying 'There's no excuse' and then doing whatever was necessary to achieve what you had set out to do, which was to submit a winning proposal."

"I sure can," said Albert. "In fact, I even made an excuse for making the excuse! I said it was the time pressure that kept us from going around the computer problem, but in reality, it was just us trying to do things the easy way."

"There will always be pressure to do the easy wrong rather than the hard right, Albert. But developing the habit of saying 'There's no excuse' will make it much easier to choose the hard right in the future. And your results will improve dramatically."

Amazing, thought Albert. *It seems so simple in many ways, but it sure is a far cry from what I've been doing.*

But rather than wonder why this represented such a difference, Albert visualized how he would enter it into his computer when he got home.

The second Winning Habit:

Never trade results for excuses.

Albert's mind was spinning as the Admiral deftly guided the immaculate yacht back to its mooring. Before he realized it, the boat was neatly tucked away with all lines secured. Albert faced the Admiral as they both stood together on the dock.

"So what are you thinking, Albert?"

"I've got some changes to make, for sure," replied Albert. "But you said there were more than two habits I should learn."

"There are, indeed," said the Admiral. "But two's enough for now. You work on these for a month. That's a fair amount of time to create a new comfort zone for yourself with these two. Then we'll get together again and see how you're doing. If you're ready for more, I'll give you more. You see, Albert, it's not enough just to learn about these things; you have to apply them to your everyday life or they won't do you a bit of good. That's one reason why the training I experienced early in life was so beneficial. We had to adopt these habits or wash out."

"Sounds exactly like my predicament right now."

"Everyone has to face it sooner or later," agreed the Admiral. "So let's move ahead with resolve, but don't try to rush it. I'd like you to keep track of how many times during the next month you have a choice to act according to these habits or do something else."

"Should I write them down?" asked Albert.

"Every day," responded the Admiral. "Keep a journal. At the end of each day, take a few minutes to review your day and note all the times when you either applied the habits, or could have and didn't. Make a note about what you'll do differently the next day, and then check the following day to make sure you did what you said you'd do."

"That's easy enough," said Albert.

"We'll see," replied the Admiral. "Bring your journal with you in four weeks and we'll see how you're doing."

"I will, sir. And thank you very much."

"You're welcome, Albert. And if you want, you can bring your bride with you next time. I hear she's a talented young woman."

"I'd like that," replied Albert with a smile. "And I know she would, too."

When Jennifer arrived home that evening, Albert was just finishing the work of getting his computer organized to help adopt the two new habits. His first step was to set the computer so the screen saver would alternately scroll each habit across the monitor. So, if the computer sat idle for more than five minutes, the first habit would scroll as follows.

... Be first on, last off, and add extra value! ...

It would be immediately followed by the second habit, which looked like this.

... Never trade results for excuses. ...

He felt that having them in different font styles would help emblazon the phrases indelibly in his memory, thereby making it easier to internalize both concepts.

Albert also programmed the computer so that a reminder with both habits would pop up on his screen each time he booted up the computer. It also told him to check his journal to make sure he was current.

The journal Albert created on his computer, if not beautiful, was at least clever. Thinking ahead to when he would be printing it out to show to Admiral Farragut, he designed a cover with a classic picture of a nineteenth-century man-of-war struggling to survive a vicious typhoon. Its sails were tattered and torn and huge waves swept across its decks, broken up by the masts that jutted up at regular intervals amidships.

He then designed each of the thirty pages so that ***Be first on, last off, and add extra value!*** printed out across the top of each page and **Never trade results for excuses** printed across the bottom of each page.

He divided the body of each page into three sections. The top two-thirds of the page were divided vertically to create two side-by-side columns. One he labeled "Smooth sailing" and the other he labeled "Stormy seas." The bottom third formed a final section that he labeled "Charting tomorrow's course." So, when he finished, each page looked like this:

Be first on, last off, and add extra value!

Smooth sailing:	Stormy seas:

Charting tomorrow's course:

Never trade results for excuses.

Winning Habits

Albert excitedly told Jennifer all about his meeting with the Admiral and what he had learned. In doing so he also told her all about the reasons for his foul mood for the past two weeks and the real reason he had gone to see Admiral Farragut in the first place.

"I'm sorry for not telling you sooner," he said. "But I was struggling to figure out what it was, myself. Then when I was just about to lay it all out, we got into your offer, so that made the timing bad."

"I understand," she responded as they gave each other a big hug. "Anyway, it sounds like you had a great day." She was relieved and happy.

"It was easy to see why Admiral Farragut was so successful," said Albert. "He's so easy to talk to and not at all hung up on himself like you might expect."

They took Digger for a long walk while Albert continued to recount his experience with the Admiral. Mrs. O'Reilly was putting her trash out when they returned. While Albert helped, he virtually blurted out the news about his meeting with the Admiral, which pleased Mrs. O'Reilly immensely. She and Jennifer exchanged a knowing wink when they parted.

A short time later Albert and Jennifer went to bed, with Albert being more relaxed than he had been in a long time.

Winning Habits

His final thought as he dozed off was, *Tomorrow's a brand new day; the first day of the rest of my life. How do I choose to live it?* He slept all through the night.

The first week Albert was on a tear. He and Jennifer started driving to work together again, and it was Albert who was now pushing to get out the door quicker each morning. He was early to every meeting. He was also the last to leave. In everything he did, he always did something extra. On Thursday, he was working on a project with a Friday deadline. Late that afternoon the main server on the computer broke down, preventing him from accessing critical information he needed to complete the project. Thinking *Never trade results for excuses* and quietly saying to himself *Damn the torpedoes,* Albert went on a mission that lasted until 1:00 A.M. Friday to get the necessary information another way and complete the project on time with all the right components.

He went to bed Friday night feeling good about himself. Saturday morning, after he and Jennifer took Digger for a romp in the park, he turned to his computer and opened his journal. It looked great. The "Smooth sailing" section on each page was filled to capacity, and there were very few listings on each page under "Stormy seas." He felt he had done a reasonable job with charting a new course each day. *Maybe,* he thought, *for the next week's journal pages I should enlarge the "Smooth sailing" section and shrink the "Stormy seas" section.*

But then he started feeling uneasy. A sort of queasiness developed in his stomach, and he noticed he wasn't feeling as good about himself as he would like. *Why am I feeling this way?* he asked himself.

Haven't I been doing a good job? Am I being honest?

Yes, he answered himself. *I have been doing what I'm supposed to, and it has felt good.*

Then what's wrong? He struggled to determine why all of a sudden he was having this anxiety attack.

Finally the reason for his discomfort began to take shape in his mind. *I've been making all these changes—doing things totally differently—and no one has noticed. No one—especially my boss—has said anything, nor is anyone acting any differently toward me.*

The disillusionment set in big time. *What good does it do to make all these changes and go to all this trouble if no one else notices?* thought Albert. He was bummed.

Just then Jennifer walked in. "Let's go down to the French Cafe for some cappuccino and brunch."

"This isn't going to work," Albert blurted back.

Winning Habits

"What?"

"This whole changing habits thing."

"What do you mean?" she asked as she plopped down in the chair next to the desk.

"It's just not going to work," he repeated.

"I don't understand. You've been going like crazy all week. It looks to me like it's working," she observed.

"Well, I'm doing everything I'm supposed to be doing, but it's not making a difference."

"What kind of difference?"

"Nobody else is doing anything differently. People haven't said anything. Nothing's changed around me."

"*I've* noticed," said Jennifer.

"That's different," argued Albert.

"And *you've* noticed," she shot back.

"So what? Don't you get it? Everyone else just thinks I'm the same old me. They're not going to change."

"What do you want them to do?"

"I don't know, but I thought I'd at least get some kind of acknowledgment or feedback that they noticed and thought it was a change for the better."

Winning Habits

"Really?"

"Well at least I didn't expect to get no response whatsoever."

"Albert, these are the kind of changes that people will acknowledge over a longer period of time. You're expecting too much, too quick. It's only been a week."

"I don't think I'm expecting a lot," said Albert.

"People aren't as focused on things like this as you think they might be. They might just discount one week's behavior as a mood swing, an energy surge, or one too many high-octane coffee beans in your cappuccino."

"But still, wouldn't at least one person say something positive?"

"Did someone say something negative?"

"No."

"Then don't fill in the blanks with negatives. You have a choice. You can fill in the blanks with positives or negatives. Think positive and you'll feel positive. Think negative and you'll feel negative. Give it time. Besides, your goal isn't to get people talking about it; your goals are to give people confidence that you're one of those people the Admiral talked about and to set yourself up for a healthy career, right? What did he call those people?"

"Pacesetters."

"That's it. It seems to me that pacesetters are in it for the long haul, not just for what people might say in a week."

"Maybe," replied Albert.

"Think positive about it," she said. "In the meantime, let's go to the French Cafe. I'm starved."

During the second week, with Jennifer's help, Albert gradually worked through his disillusionment. He continued to complete his journal each day. And even though he didn't put forth the same level of energy and wild enthusiasm that he had initially, he still stuck with it.

During the third week, Albert became more comfortable with the changes he was making. They started becoming second nature. And with Jennifer still giving him strong support, he continued to apply his new practices.

By the time the fourth week came around, Albert was completely comfortable with his newly acquired habits. They were becoming as much a part of him as any element of his personality.

And then it happened.

On Thursday afternoon one of Albert's project teams held a meeting to celebrate the accomplishment of their first major milestone and review the team's progress. At the end of the meeting, Susan asked permission to speak. "I think everyone has done a great job," she said. "But I want to especially acknowledge the extra effort Albert has put in during the past few weeks."

"Hear, hear," said Whitney. "If it hadn't been for his diligence and commitment to stay ahead of things, we'd never have made our goal on time."

"Bravo!" exclaimed Carl.

"That's really true," said Ron, the project team leader. "If it wasn't for all the extra value Albert added, we'd be struggling to catch up."

"I think you've just given us a great new nickname for Albert," said Susan. "I say from here on out we call him Value-Added Albert."

"Hear, hear," said Whitney.

"Bravo!" said Carl.

"Done," declared Ron.

The glow of that moment lasted for a couple of days. Albert appreciated the team's comments, and he took pride in his new nickname. But the more he reflected on their remarks, the more his focus shifted inward. He began to appreciate what he was doing for himself. Not only did he trust that the long-term payoff would eventually come, but he simply felt better about himself because of his new habits. He felt he was contributing more and accomplishing more without all that much extra effort. He was working smarter, not harder. He felt more rewarded and productive personally. That's what really felt good. He felt like he had increased his value as a person. At least to himself, anyway. He'd find out later if anyone else agreed with him. *But it would be hard to disagree,* he thought. *The facts, in terms of the results I'm producing, pretty much speak for themselves.*

Albert found himself looking forward to the following Sunday's meeting with the Admiral like a five-year-old looks forward to a birthday party.

Jennifer was also excited about meeting Admiral Farragut, partly because of his reputation and partly because of the profound changes he had caused in Albert.

So on Sunday Albert and Jennifer went to church, then to brunch, and arrived at the marina a few minutes early. As they walked down the dock toward the yacht, they didn't realize that the Admiral had exited the harbor master's hut after they walked past it and had fallen into step behind them. When he announced his presence about halfway down the pier, it startled them both.

"Hah!" he exclaimed. "Well, I see you've internalized the first habit."

Winning Habits

"Oh, Admiral Farragut," Albert responded as he stopped walking and turned around. The two shook hands. He wasn't sure how to respond to the Admiral's statement.

"Job well done," said the Admiral. "Or, as we used to say in the fleet, Bravo Zulu to you."

Albert responded with a puzzled look on his face.

"The first habit—'first on and last off.' You're here early. Slightly ahead of me, in fact. Well done."

Albert blushed slightly, obviously a bit flustered. He hadn't realized what he had done.

"No sense being uncomfortable about it. That's the way it should be. And this must be the wonderful Jennifer I've heard so much about from Mrs. O'Reilly."

It was Jennifer's turn to be a bit flustered, meeting the famed Admiral for the first time. Speechlessly, she extended her hand.

The Admiral shook it warmly and said, "What say we get on board and get this afternoon underway?"

"Sounds great to me," responded Jennifer, regaining her composure.

Quick as a flash they were aboard the Admiral's yacht. Jennifer looked around, every bit as impressed by the perfect condition of the yacht as Albert had been during his first trip.

Winning Habits

"Is that your journal, Albert?" the Admiral asked, glancing down to the folder Albert was carrying.

"Yes, sir," Albert responded, as he offered it to the Admiral.

The Admiral skimmed through it. "Clever," he observed. "I figured you must have done a good job with it, or you wouldn't have picked up the habits. So, fill me in on how it went."

With Jennifer's help, Albert recounted the previous month's efforts, telling how he had started enthusiastically, had become disillusioned, and then had proceeded to the present with Jennifer's support, feeling he had changed in a truly positive and lasting way.

"Everyone has ups and downs with these things. Your experience was fairly typical."

"There were a few times when my commitment was really tested," said Albert.

"I'm sure," responded the Admiral. "But how does it feel now?"

"Great. I'm glad I stuck with it."

"So am I," interjected Jennifer. "I think Albert's going to be a lot happier in the future. But I benefited as well. Those were habits I practiced sometimes, but not as consistently as I should have. That's because I never really thought about them or knew why I behaved that way when I did. But talking about them and working on them with Albert helped make them more explicit in my mind, so it's helped me improve, too. I'm much better off because I've learned more about them."

"Good," declared the Admiral. "Well, are you ready to take on a couple more?"

"Sure," the pair responded in unison.

"There's no sense talking about all this stuff here at the dock when we could be out on the water enjoying one of God's greatest blessings. Let's get underway, and then we'll talk."

They quickly completed the necessary rituals, and in no time at all were headed out of the marina and into San Diego Harbor.

Once they were out on the open water, the Admiral spoke. "The first two habits I taught you were enabling or 'shaping up' habits. By that I mean they set you up so you could do something else to produce great results. In other words, you're first on and last off so you can produce some other result. You don't accept any excuses for *the result* you are trying to produce. The habits aren't the end; they are a *means* to a better end. By themselves they don't produce results."

Jennifer and Albert nodded their understanding.

Winning Habits

"The next habit focuses more directly on results. But before we talk about it, there are a few things we need to understand. Fair enough?"

The couple nodded again.

"First we're going to talk about problems and decisions. And the first thing I want you both to realize is that most problems are the result of solutions!" The Admiral stopped talking and gazed out over the water as he stood behind the wheel, keeping the yacht on an even keel.

Finally Albert broke the silence. "You mean that when you solve one problem, you're likely to create others."

"Every move's a move, and everything you do makes a difference. But not every difference you make is intended. Or even positive, for that matter. More often than not, when people decide to do something—either to implement a new decision or to solve a problem—they create unintended consequences. Those unintended consequences are new problems."

"When you stop and think about it, it does make a lot of sense," said Albert.

"Think of some of the problems that have frustrated you in your company recently. I'll bet most of them wouldn't have become problems if someone hadn't taken action to solve another problem earlier."

"Just last week," said Jennifer, "we changed our project reporting requirements because of some information that the finance department needed to capture. When we made the changes, they wreaked havoc for the sales and marketing forecasts that the VP of sales has to create. We solved finance's problems and created one for sales."

"It happens all the time," observed the Admiral.

"So how can you avoid it?" asked Albert.

"By troubleshooting your action plans before you implement them."

"Troubleshooting?" asked Jennifer.

"Yes, troubleshooting. In fact, troubleshooting is the essence of the third winning habit, which is *Solve problems in advance.*" The words lit up in Albert's mind.

Albert took out the folder containing his journal and wrote the habit on the inside flap the way he would enter it into his computer when he got home.

The third Winning Habit:

Solve problems in advance.

When he finished writing he turned back to the Admiral. "How do we make this a habit?"

Winning Habits

"Hah!" exclaimed the Admiral. "Good question, because this one's harder than the first two. You can't make anticipatory problem solving a habit unless you learn to troubleshoot your decisions. You also have to learn how to troubleshoot solutions to the problems you solve. But you can't do either of those unless you first have figured out a logical and consistent method for solving problems and making decisions."

"Do you have a good method?" asked Albert. *Dumb question,* he immediately thought to himself. But, catching himself thinking negatively, he quickly added, *Maybe he has more than one good method.*

"Yep. And it's a good one."

"We could sure use it," said Jennifer. "A lot of times when we work on problems together we get frustrated because we each approach the problem differently. But it's not just us; the same thing happens to everyone else at work, too."

"The problem-solving and decision-making method I use has been tried and proved by managers around the world. I like it because it's practical and designed for everyday use by people working in organizations. You can use it for both problems and decisions, and it applies to every type of problem you'll encounter on the job."

"Almost sounds too good to be true," observed Jennifer.

"It's also jargon free, which is what I like," said the Admiral. "Some of these approaches have so much special language in them that you almost have to learn a new vocabulary before you can start to use the method. But the two things I like most about it are first, that it focuses on results, and second, that it is anticipatory—meaning that it relies on a troubleshooting step that forces you to identify potential problems you might create *before* you implement your solution."

"This is exciting," said Jennifer.

"Let's come about, and then I'll explain it to you," he said as he turned the wheel to port.

"Watch your heads," the Admiral directed as the yacht started coming about and the boom swept across the cockpit. In a moment he had the boat steadied on a new heading.

"Here, Mr. Value-Added Albert. You take the helm and keep her on this track while I lay this out on the back of your folder there."

Albert slipped in behind the wheel and the Admiral took the seat next to Jennifer. He removed a nylon-tipped pen from the pocket of his windbreaker and quickly jotted the seven-step process on the back of the folder.

Decision Making	*Problem Solving*
	Define the Problem
Define Objective(s)	Define Objective(s)
Generate Alternatives	Generate Alternatives
Develop Action Plan	Develop Action Plan
Troubleshoot	Troubleshoot
Communicate	Communicate
Implement	Implement

Winning Habits

"Note that you follow all seven steps when solving problems. When you're merely making a decision, you use only the last six steps."

"I see," said Jennifer.

"Or put another way, you use the six steps for decision making. Then when a problem arises, you define the problem and then use those same six steps to decide what to do with it."

"Neat," observed Albert from behind the wheel.

"Now here's something else," explained the Admiral as he flipped over the folder and sketched out a different representation of the method on the back side.

While he wrote, he continued his explanation. "The first four steps—down to and including 'Develop Action Plan'—focus on arriving at the desired *answer*; the last three steps—'Troubleshoot,' 'Communicate,' and 'Implement'—focus on ensuring that the desired *result* is produced."

The couple continued to listen intently.

"You see," explained the Admiral, "answers and results aren't always the same. And answers don't count unless they lead to the right result. Here's what it looks like."

He held the folder up for both to see.

Step One	**Define the Problem**
Plus,	
Step Two	**Define Objective(s)**
Plus,	
Step Three	**Generate Alternatives**
Plus,	
Step Four	**Develop Action Plan**
EQUALS = The Right Answer,	
Plus,	
Step Five	**Troubleshoot**
Plus,	
Step Six	**Communicate**
Plus,	
Step Seven	**Implement**
EQUALS = The Right Result.	

"Fascinating," said Jennifer. "Could you please tell us in your words what each of the seven steps is about?"

"Be glad to," declared the Admiral.

"May I have Albert's journal while you explain?" she asked. "I'd like to take notes on the back of his journal pages so we can capture all this."

"Good idea," said Albert as Jennifer took the journal pages out of the folder. She let the Admiral keep the folder so that he could refer to it as he completed his explanation. Once she was organized, the Admiral began.

"Let's start with *Define the Problem*. In organizations, problems are either obstacles or deviations. An obstacle prevents the outcome you desire. A deviation is an outcome different from what you desire. The first step in problem solving is to understand what the problem is and to define the problem clearly so that others can also understand what it is. A problem has both a cause and an effect." As he wrote on the inside back of the folder, he said, "A simple definition of a problem might follow this general format:"

A (something)

is causing

B (some undesirable effect).

"So," he said, "if you follow this format, an example of a specific problem might sound like this:"

He held up the folder and pointed to A, saying, "Fred's continual failure to submit information promptly to me ..."

Pointing to B, he continued, "... is causing ...

"...my late completion and filing of my reports," he finished.

"I'm with you," said Jennifer as Albert nodded agreement.

"To check your definition of a problem, be sure that it describes both a cause and an effect," continued the Admiral. "Remember that the definition of a problem describes only an undesirable effect and its cause—the definition doesn't imply solutions."

Jennifer hurriedly wrote down this important point.

"That takes us to the next step. The first step in decision making and the second step in problem solving is to *Define Objectives*: that is, define the outcome you would like to achieve as a result of solving the problem or making the decision. Objectives specify only the outcome you would like to achieve. The action plan, which is developed in step four, specifies the means by which you hope to achieve this outcome. An objective might follow this format:"

Again he outlined a format on the folder, underlining key words.

To *action verb*

single key result

by *date*

at *cost.*

"The objective could be an action you want to take, or it could be an action you want someone else to take. For example, a clear definition of objectives for the specific problem with Fred might read:

"*To ensure* that Fred submits the information I need ..." he recited, emphasizing the key words he had underlined on the folder,

"... *by* the tenth of the month ...

"... *at* no additional cost."

"*To ensure* that I submit my reports ...

"...*by* the fifteenth of each month ...

"... *at* no additional cost."

Winning Habits

"Of course, the number and format of objectives may vary according to the definition of the problem and your priorities, but you will find this simple format to be a good starting point."

"This is really good stuff," observed Jennifer.

"The next step is the solution-generating step of the process—*Generate Alternatives*. In this step you generate as many alternative ways as you can to achieve the objectives you defined in the previous step. For example, if you were to generate alternative ways to solve the problem with Fred, you might compile a list," he said, ticking off the following:

- Discuss the problem with Fred.
- Discuss the problem with my boss.
- Discuss the problem with Fred's boss.
- Write Fred a memo asking for his cooperation.
- Ask for a transfer.
- Reorganize so I don't have to rely on Fred.
- Ask that Fred be transferred.
- Ask that Fred be fired.
- Do nothing.
- Submit the reports without Fred's input, stating that the reason for doing this was his failure to cooperate.

- Submit a written complaint to Fred's department head.
- Submit a written complaint to my boss.
- Threaten Fred.
- Resign.

"That's a long list," observed Jennifer when she was sure the Admiral had finished.

"And some of those alternatives are not good ones. However, at this point, generating as many alternatives as you can is useful, because some that aren't good may lead you to others that are. Remember that in this step you are only generating alternatives—not evaluating them or selecting them."

"Then what do you do?" asked Albert.

"You *Develop an Action Plan*," answered the Admiral. "This step has two phases. First, you evaluate the alternatives you generated in the previous step to choose one or more as your solution. Second, you modify the chosen alternative(s) until an action plan is fully developed."

He outlined a simple action plan that might be used in the early stages of Fred's problem:

1. Talk to my boss first; explain my problem with Fred and what I intend to do about it.

2. Talk to Fred, addressing the following:
   —the impact of his behavior on me
   —the impact of his behavior on the organization
   —the desired behavior
   —the consequences of continuing on
   —the consequences of acting as desired
3. Report the results of my conversation with Fred to my boss.
4. Provide Fred with performance-based feedback regarding his subsequent behavior.

"So you don't necessarily have to use the alternatives exactly the way they were created when you brainstormed them," observed Jennifer.

"That's right. You use them as a basis for a comprehensive action plan that makes sense, given your objectives. You will often add even more alternatives during the action-planning step."

"That takes us to troubleshooting," observed Albert.

"Good," said the Admiral. "You two catch on quick. Now remember what we said earlier. Most problems are the result of solutions and decisions. The best way to avoid these additional, unintended problems is to *Troubleshoot* your action plan before you implement it. Troubleshooting the action plan is the most cost-effective and efficient problem solving you can perform as a manager. Solving problems before they happen is the best problem solving possible."

"Wait a minute while I get all that," requested Jennifer, madly scribbling away.

"This is the tie-in to the third secret," interjected Albert. "Most of the time that you'll be solving problems in advance is when you're solving other problems."

"That's right," said the Admiral. "Always review your solutions or intended action plan in terms of the future and try to anticipate potential problems. Then modify your action plan to solve these problems or bypass them before they occur or before they become potential crises. In trouble-shooting your action plan for the problem with Fred, you might anticipate some of these potential problems:

1. Fred may not respond to your discussion.
2. Fred may go to his department head and complain that you are harassing him.
3. Your boss may tell you to leave Fred alone.

"And I'm sure you can think of other potential problems. As the problem solver you must decide which of these are serious enough to warrant your modifying the action plan.

For those that are less serious, you may simply develop contingency plans."

"So I could even go back and modify my objectives based on potential problems I hadn't thought of until now," observed Jennifer.

"Yep," acknowledged the Admiral. "And the more you use the method, the more adept you'll get at it. Pretty soon it will become second nature to you."

"I'm already thinking about how I'm going to handle some things differently using this method," said Albert from behind the wheel.

"Great," said the Admiral. "Then let's talk about the next step: *Communicate*. In this step you determine which individuals or groups might affect the success of your action plan. Then you determine the best method for giving them the best information to ensure the success of your action plan. You can choose from many methods of communicating to everyone the information you want them to have: for example, personal visits, telephone calls, memos, letters, audio tapes, videotapes, and computer messages. For different people, you will need to specify different communication objectives. For the problem with Fred, you might outline a simple plan such as this." Again he wrote on the folder.

Person	Objective	Method
My Boss	**Seek Advice**	**Personal Visit**
	Gain Support	
Fred	**Change Behavior**	**Personal Visit**
	Meet Deadlines	
	Seek Future Cooperation	

"Even though these both focus on individuals, for some problems you might focus on a group of people?" asked Jennifer.

"Exactly. Or a market, or a company, or whatever population you might need to act in unison. But don't focus on a group communication objective when you want different people in the group to act differently. In those cases target each individual separately."

"Got it," said Jennifer, still furiously taking notes.

"Which leaves only *Implementation*," observed the Admiral. "I shouldn't say *only* implementation, though, because this final step in problem solving and decision making involves more than merely *starting* the action. You haven't solved a problem or made a successful decision until you have achieved all the objectives you have defined. Therefore, implementation includes follow-up and monitoring through the completion of every objective your action plan specifies. In the case of the problem with Fred, *starting* the action is simple. But follow-up and monitoring Fred's behavior will be an important part of implementation."

"This looks like powerful stuff," said Albert. "I can already see where I'll be able to use it on a lot of my projects."

"It's a practical way to organize projects," agreed the Admiral. "And it's a powerful way to outline project proposals and reports for better communication, too. But the most important secret here is to remember to troubleshoot whenever possible. That means making problem solving in advance a habit."

"Our third secret. I'm sure there's a lot more we should know about this, isn't there?" asked Jennifer.

"More than fifty percent of all failures occur because of foreseeable problems that the implementers failed to foresee. Remember when I told you most problems are the result of solutions?"

"Sure do."

"Well, because we've grown up in an answer-oriented society, most people believe that coming up with a good answer is enough. But remember, in management—or any work you do in organizations—having the right answer is never enough. It's producing the right results that counts."

"I see," said Jennifer.

"When a good answer meets an unexpected negative event, the result is usually a negative outcome. More often than not, the negative outcome is a problem or series of problems that causes the objective to be missed."

"So that's where troubleshooting comes in," piped up Albert. "Figure out what all the unexpected—or I guess maybe even expected—problems might be and change your action plan before implementing it in order to avoid more problems."

"That's it," said the Admiral. "You make so many decisions during the course of a day that you won't be able to use the seven-step method formally every time. But once you've used it a few times, it will become a mental roadmap you can follow almost subconsciously with each decision or problem."

"A problem-solving paradigm," observed Jennifer.

"Your term, not mine," responded the Admiral. "But I guess it works. My point is that the mental map most people follow is more like this: evaluate quickly, decide, and then do! They leave out several key steps that make a huge difference to their eventual results. First, they don't think about what their new objective should be. Second, they rarely consider enough alternatives—you can always improve upon the first solution that comes to mind. And I think most important, they don't anticipate potential problems and deal with them. So they set themselves up for disaster."

"In order to avoid disaster, think troubleshoot," said Jennifer.

"It's fairly easy to develop the habit of always pausing a second before taking action to ask yourself what might go wrong," said the Admiral. "It's the longcut that will always turn out to be the shortcut in the long run."

"And I can see how it helps you to be prepared," said Albert.

"Except troubleshooting is not all there is to being prepared, Albert."

"What do you mean?" asked Albert.

Winning Habits

"They're related, but somewhat different. Let me share an example, and then we'll talk about it."

"We're all ears," said Jennifer.

"My brother-in-law had a successful career as a trial lawyer. At one time during his career he won forty-seven consecutive civil cases that he took to trial. Given the idiosyncrasies of our legal system, that's quite a feat. Most people consider a fifty percent success rate to be good."

"That's fabulous," said Jennifer. "And I'll bet the reason he was so successful was that he was prepared each time."

"It wasn't so much that he *was* prepared," explained the Admiral. "Every lawyer prepares to go to trial. It was in *how* he prepared."

"What was his secret?" asked Albert.

"I discovered it one day when we were together at a birthday party for Mrs. O'Reilly. He had just won the biggest case of his career. It was well publicized and the newspapers had been covering it for weeks. He won the jury over at the last minute with a phenomenal courtroom performance that will be used as a case study in law schools for years to come. A reporter wrote in a newspaper that he had 'pulled a rabbit out of the hat' at the most critical point in the trial."

"So it was almost like magic," observed Albert.

"That's the way it appeared to everyone, including me. Then at Mrs. O'Reilly's party I asked him how he did it—how he always managed to pull the rabbit out of the hat at exactly the right moment."

"What did he say?" asked Jennifer.

"He said the secret to pulling the right rabbit out of the hat at the right moment was to always make sure he had at least ten rabbits in the hat! *That* was his secret and *that* was the kind of preparation he thrived on."

"What did he do with the other nine?" asked Albert.

"Nothing. Except learn an awful lot from them. It made him smarter the next time. But at the same time it made him a better troubleshooter as well. The common denominator for troubleshooting and being prepared is that both rely on anticipatory thinking. But it's easier to think about trouble-shooting and being prepared than to remember anticipatory thinking."

"Wow," exclaimed Jennifer and Albert in unison.

"A lot of people thought my brother-in-law was lucky. It wasn't luck so much as preparation. He *planned* on pulling rabbits out of the hat. But there was only one way he could guarantee having the right one available at the right time. He anticipated every problem he might encounter during the trial and solved each one in advance—before the trial started. Those solutions became the rabbits he loaded into the hat."

"It seems so obvious," said Albert. "So simple. Yet I don't know anyone who does it."

"Some of the better salespeople do it. They try to anticipate objections they might encounter before going into a sales meeting. Outside of salespeople, though, I don't know many who do it, even though the opportunities abound. It's one of life's ironies, young man. But it's no different from the other habits, is it? The secret is to live them. A lot of people have heard many of these secrets before. They can even cite examples where they've seen them work. But then they pooh-pooh ideas like these because they want life to be more complicated. I think some people are afraid to face the fact that most of life's winning secrets are more simple than complex. The secret isn't in figuring out and mastering some complex and difficult equation; it's in applying these straightforward truths to your everyday life. Again, I'll use my brother-in-law as an example. He said he shared his secret with everyone—didn't try to hide it at all. In spite of his record, how many people do you think ever followed his lead?"

"How many?" asked Albert.

"He said as far as he was able to tell, none."

"Amazing," observed Jennifer.

Winning Habits

"It's one reason why I wanted to see if Albert was going to apply the first two secrets before I bothered to share the second two with him," explained the Admiral. "No sense wasting my time on someone who won't use what I have to offer. And it'd be a waste of time for you, too, Albert. Because if you're not willing to do the first secret, you'll never develop the habit of doing the third one, will you?"

"Probably not," said Albert.

"Hah!" exclaimed the Admiral.

"Wow, that reminds me," said Albert. "*Solve problems in advance* is only the third secret. I mean it's a great one and all that, but we still have one more secret to learn."

"I think you're doing great so far," said the Admiral. "Anytime you're ready we can go on to the fourth and final secret."

Albert and Jennifer looked at each other and answered in unison. "We're ready."

"The fourth secret is a little trickier than the other three, because people usually don't see it as a habit at first. First let me tell you how I learned about it, then I'll tell you what it is."

"Sounds good," said Albert. "But before we get started, do you think we ought to change course here?"

"Almost lost track of things," said the Admiral. "Go ahead and bring her about to port. I'll ease up on this line here, and then you bring us about. Good. Now we'll duck." The boom swung across the cockpit as the opposite side of the sails filled with air. "See, you really are Value-Added Albert."

Albert smiled and steadied on the new course as the Admiral continued.

"Early on in my career I was attending postgraduate school. As part of the curriculum, each month the school brought in a distinguished guest speaker. We'd listen to what the speaker had to say and then have the opportunity for questions and answers after the conclusion of the talk. One month they had this young guy who had been a phenomenal success in the electronic media. Radio and TV were the hot things back then. Those companies were going gangbusters and they created a lot of opportunity for talented people who wanted to go places in their careers."

"Must have been like the Internet now," said Albert.

"Exactly. Well, this young man—and I mean young; he even looked young to me and I was only a lieutenant at the time—had gone right to the top of the leading company in the industry. So we heard him talk and it was interesting. But the most interesting part came at the end when he opened it up for questions. One of the first questions he was asked was how he had reached the top at such an early age. I mean, here he was, probably not even forty years old and sitting on top of an industry giant that was a household name. So we were all curious to know how he had bypassed so many people and made it all the way to the top so quickly."

"What was his answer?" asked Albert.

"Well, it knocked my socks off," said the Admiral. "But I'm not so sure too many people got the full meaning of it."

"I think you get a lot of things most people don't," observed Jennifer.

"He said he hadn't spent a lot of time dwelling on the subject, but he had given the question some thought in the past. He said he attributed his success and rapid rise to the top to three things. First, he said he had always done everything possible in every job he ever held to make his boss and his boss's boss and those above him in the organization look good. No-brainer, right?" asked the Admiral. "But it didn't stop there. Second, he said he could honestly look himself in the mirror and say that in every job he ever held he had always done everything possible to make his *subordinates* look good. But it didn't stop there, either. Finally, he said he honestly believed that in every job he had ever held he truly believed he had done everything possible to make his colleagues and co-workers—his *peers* in the organization—look good. He said the rest was easy. With everyone around him going up, he just went with the flow!"

"Wow again," said Albert. "But it sounds a little manipulative."

Winning Habits

"Until you fully understand it," said the Admiral. "But once you do, you'll find a world of wisdom in those words. First let me explain the part about making everyone look good. He didn't mean to do it artificially—to make everyone look good when they hadn't done anything to earn it. Rather, he meant to first find out what results they were trying to produce, to understand their goals and objectives and the challenges they faced, and then find ways to help them achieve their purposes in the best possible manner *without* trying to take any of the credit away from them. In other words, make them truly look good. Find ways to support them, and let them have all the credit."

"When you think about it," observed Jennifer, "letting them have all the credit is just supporting them on another level."

"That's good!" exclaimed the Admiral.

"And then when those around you move up, you'll go with the flow?" asked Albert.

"Hah! But think about it. Our young executive didn't just go with the flow. He dramatically *exceeded* the flow. He moved up faster than anyone else. And it's important to understand why."

"You'll have to help me," said Albert.

"Think for a moment about all the people you work with in whatever is a reasonably sized work group. Maybe it's your department, maybe it's a group of colleagues who do the same kind of work you do, or maybe it's a project team you've been part of for a while. The important thing is that you think of a group of people with whom you have fairly frequent contact."

"Okay," said Albert.

"Got a group in mind?" the Admiral asked Jennifer.

"Got it."

"Okay. Now think of all the members of that group. Do you know who the consistent contributors are? Do you know who is more reliable and who is less reliable? Do you know who always carries their weight and who skates regularly? Do you know most members' strengths and weaknesses? Good habits and bad?"

"I think so," said Jennifer.

"Pretty much," responded Albert.

"Hah!" exclaimed the Admiral. "And so does everyone else."

Jennifer and Albert both wanted to share the Admiral's enthusiasm for the point, but they couldn't because they didn't get it.

"Don't you see? The point is that everyone knows. If you were to survey everyone in each of those groups confidentially and have them rank everyone else in the group according to their level of contribution,

everyone's list would be the same. Everyone knows who contributes most and who contributes least. No one fools everyone for too long, and the truth always prevails."

Jennifer and Albert were still a bit puzzled.

"You never have to seek recognition—especially public recognition—because everyone who matters knows the truth anyway over time. And ultimately the truth will drive their decisions. This is exactly what happened with the young executive. He didn't try to take credit for the accomplishments of his boss, even though he contributed significantly to them. Nor did he compete for recognition with his subordinates or peers. He did everything possible to help them succeed and to get them fair public recognition for their success. But deep down inside they all knew he had helped them immensely.

"So the end result was that they all wanted to work with him. Subordinates fought to be able to work for him because he always supported them and helped publicly celebrate their victories. They took pride in seeing their efforts rewarded. Peers wanted him on their team for the same reason. And it's obvious why leaders sought him out—they never felt threatened and they appreciated his loyalty. His unselfish attitude and total support for those around him created a demand for him in the company that propelled him to the top in record time."

"But didn't some people get jealous and try to run him down or ruin his reputation?" asked Albert.

"I'm sure they did. There will always be people who think the best way to get ahead is to push others back. But it didn't work, did it? Because sooner or later everyone knows. That's the key. The most important thing to understand is that at some point, everyone knows. Once you understand that, then you can apply the fourth secret, which by now you can probably guess. It's to develop the habit of always making those around you look good."

Albert quickly pictured what it would look like on his computer at home.

The fourth Winning Habit:

Always make those around you look good.

Then a sudden realization drew him quickly back into reality.

"As I think about all you've just said, it's easy for me to see another of the reasons Jennifer has been promoted and I haven't," observed Albert.

The comment made Jennifer feel uncomfortable, but she didn't say anything. She didn't like getting into comparisons of the two of them. But the Admiral seemed pleased that Albert had raised the issue.

Winning Habits

"Tell us about it," said the Admiral.

"One way to say it is that Jennifer is more of a contributor than me," stated Albert. "My attitude has typically been more of a 'get the job done' approach and hers is always more of a 'let's do what's best' attitude."

"But I think I'm a long way away from the young executive," said Jennifer.

"Not compared to me," countered Albert. "Even though I get along with people, I've never given much thought to trying to make them look good. At least you are always trying to pull them into things and make it a group effort."

"It does sound like you've got at least a bit of a head start, Jennifer," observed the Admiral.

"Maybe. But I think I've got a long way to go before I can compare myself to the young executive you described. I've never even thought about a lot of that stuff before."

"You'll both have some fun working on this one. And if you're at all like me, you'll experience some frustrations along the way. For example, you will encounter selfish people, and sometimes it won't seem fair to you to always want to give the credit to others. But in the end you'll feel better about yourself, and you'll find it will have been a much more satisfying and rewarding path to follow."

"Please tell us about one of the frustrating experiences you had with this secret and how you overcame it," asked Albert.

"I can do that," responded the Admiral. "Just as soon as we make one more turn here and head back toward home. Let's bring her around and head about yon," he said, pointing in the general direction of the marina.

As soon as they settled in on the new course, the Admiral traded places with Albert and once again took the helm.

"The most challenging time came right after I left the Navy. I was asked to take over as Executive Vice President of a major nonprofit organization. I had been recruited by a number of firms—a few defense contractors, some high-tech startups, some lobbying and international relations firms, even a few investment banking companies. But I wanted to do something significant, and I saw my opportunity with this outfit.

"During the recruiting process, I told the organization's CEO all about my ideas and he seemed receptive. He said if I came to work with him I'd have the opportunity to pursue my lofty ambitions and make a difference in the world. I wanted an opportunity to pursue my dreams, so when he said he supported them, I took him at his word. I believed he wanted to be supportive and help me realize my vision.

"But I was wrong. The real reason he wanted to hire me was to give himself more credibility. He was having problems. His pet programs were on the rocks and he lacked the ability to salvage them. He was more concerned about image than substance and thought that bringing in someone with my experience to work for him would turn things around. But deep down inside I really think he felt as though he'd hired a 'blue chip' scapegoat. I think he felt secure putting me in the Executive VP position so that when his projects crashed and burned—which he believed they would—he could blame it all on me. He'd be able to say 'It was Farragut's fault' or 'If Farragut couldn't make it work, no one could,' and save his own keester in the process.

"So the week I came on board, he said things had changed since we talked earlier. He told me I couldn't implement any of my ideas, but would have to work on his crippled programs."

"What did you do?" asked Jennifer. "Did you resign?"

"No, but I knew I'd been had. That first weekend was a tough one. My dear wife Amelia, God rest her soul, told me to get out while the getting was good. She strongly urged me to take one of the other offers and let this guy ride his own sinking ship to the watery depths.

"But I thought about it for a while and finally said, 'Damn the torpedoes, this is for the kids in the world! We're just going to have to make it work.' So I took on that assignment—one that no one else in his right mind would have taken. And I committed to make it work.

Winning Habits

"I worked morning, noon, and night. But it wasn't just me. As always happens, it was a whole group of us that ended up saving it. Anyway, he had three programs that were sinking fast. We turned all three around. And when we did, I made sure that he got all the credit. Amelia said she always suspected I was at least a half a bubble off and now this proved it! It really upset her that the team and I put all that effort into a task that was next to impossible and then gave the credit away. When I told her he deserved the credit because, after all, he was the one who hired me, she still wasn't satisfied."

"I think I agree with your wife," said Jennifer.

"Sorry, but me too," added Albert.

"That's because you haven't heard the end of the story. Hah! The impatience of youth."

"What happened next?" asked Jennifer.

"Well, he started giving all of us more freedom to do the things we wanted to do. And every time we achieved something positive, which happened more and more frequently, we saw to it that he received the credit. After all, he was the CEO and had the ultimate responsibility for the organization's successes. Within a year or two, we were on a roll."

"Then what happened?" asked Albert.

"It didn't happen all at once," explained the Admiral. "Things like this never do. But it didn't take long for the

Board of Trustees to see what was happening. And they, like everyone else in the organization, knew. They knew who was driving the results, regardless of who was taking public credit. They realized that the whole organization would be better if they made some changes. So they moved the CEO to another position on the Board and assigned him responsibilities that were more in line with his abilities. They made me the CEO, and the rest is history. We made more of a difference in the lives of kids around the world than any other organization in the history of the world."

"It had to have been hard to try to make that jerk look good," said Albert.

"But it was the only way to turn things around without making a bigger mess," explained the Admiral. "The important thing is that in the end it worked."

"But it also took a lot of courage," said Jennifer.

"Maybe," reflected the Admiral. Then, after a short pause: "I think it's also important to note that it worked because I had a higher-level goal in mind and kept focused on that goal. I could have started competing with the CEO, and maybe even won out, but that would have drained energy from my overall goal and made it much more difficult to achieve. It would have caused me to pick up at least one enemy along the way. And it could also have created a lot of negatives with other people—at least a few people would doubt whether they could ever trust me. Life should be about gaining allies, not picking up enemies."

"I don't know if I could ever do what you just described," said Jennifer.

"Me neither," said Albert.

"That's only because you've never given it much conscious thought before. And if you don't make it the focus of deliberate effort like you did for the first two habits, then you're right. You won't ever do it. But knowing the two of you, I think you'll do gangbusters."

"But I've got another question that came up while you were talking," said Albert.

"Shoot," said the Admiral.

"What do you do if one of those people around you doesn't deserve to look good?"

The Admiral answered with a question of his own. "Why would somebody *not* deserve to look good?"

"Maybe you don't get along with them. Maybe they're selfish. Maybe they've done something to you to make you look bad in the past. Maybe they're just jerks!"

"Yeah," Jennifer added, "it's not that you want to go after them or lower yourself to their level or anything like that. But because of their history, you sure don't want to make them look good. They could use it against you."

"Do it right and you won't be creating a more powerful adversary, you'll be creating an ally," declared the Admiral.

"Remember, looking good is the result of being good. Support their goals, help solve their problems, show that you truly are interested in helping them achieve in line with the overall organization's goals, and they'll become allies. Too often we think we have bad relationships with people because the people themselves are bad. Sometimes that's the case, but very rarely. When we think the people are bad, we rarely salvage the relationship. But this is a lesson you'll have to learn yourself. I can talk about it all the way across the ocean. But until you experience the power of this principle firsthand, you'll never fully appreciate it."

"It would be foolish for me to challenge you much further on this, but I've got to be honest. This is going to be a hard one for me," said Albert.

"Me, too," answered Jennifer.

"Nothing worth doing is ever easy," observed the Admiral.

"So should we keep journals for these two habits like I did for the first two?" asked Albert.

Winning Habits

"Absolutely. And remember that when you become disillusioned during your learning process, help each other work through it. That way you can continue to be each other's greatest blessing."

Before long they were back alongside the dock with everything properly stowed.

Jennifer and Albert thanked the Admiral profusely, they all promised to keep in touch, and then they said their good-byes.

On the way home they stopped and bought a beautiful bouquet of flowers for Mrs. O'Reilly along with a canister of her favorite herbal tea. As soon as they had checked on Digger, they took the gifts to Mrs. O'Reilly and spent an hour and a half enthusiastically reviewing the highlights of their time with the Admiral. Mrs. O'Reilly couldn't have been more pleased.

They were still glowing later that evening when they finally returned home and worked together to set up the computer and their new journals.

First they changed the screensaver so it would scroll the two new messages. They agreed to keep the old messages, lest they be pushed aside in their efforts to learn the new. So the screensaver now scrolled all four messages:

... Be first on, last off, and add extra value! ...

was followed by

... **Never trade results for excuses.** ...

then came

... **Solve problems in advance!** ...

and, finally,

... Always make those around you look good! ...

Both agreed that the "Smooth sailing/Stormy seas" and "Charting tomorrow's course" format would work well for these two new habits. So Albert quickly brought up a template and created a new file for both himself and Jennifer with the new habits as subheadings.

Solve problems in advance!

Smooth sailing:	Stormy seas:

Charting tomorrow's course:

Always make those around you look good!

Winning Habits

For the cover of his journal, Albert chose a picture of the space shuttle taking off, just seconds after launch, with billowing clouds of white exhaust cushioning the initial moments of what would be an exciting journey.

Jennifer chose an image of Victoria Falls taken just at sunrise, showing a beautiful rainbow in the mist created by thousands of gallons of cascading water that flowed naturally into the churning pools below.

It was well past midnight by the time they climbed exhausted into bed for one of the more peaceful night's sleep either could remember.

The next month was as satisfying as it was challenging. The first week, it seemed like anything that could go wrong did go wrong. Albert's project was cancelled because of the customer's changing priorities. Two people in Jennifer's group left—one went to a different company in another state because his wife was transferred and the other was reassigned to another group where the company felt she was more needed. By the time the next weekend rolled around, neither Albert nor Jennifer felt as though much progress had been made toward the adoption of their new habits.

It took most of the weekend to work things through and realize that the disillusionment was both natural and predictable.

Winning Habits

"It's amazing, isn't it?" remarked Jennifer. "Even though we both said we weren't going to become disillusioned, here we are. This must be what causes a lot of people to abandon their change efforts."

"This is the second time it has caused me to want to abandon mine," observed Albert.

"Well, I guess we better just get used to it," said Jennifer.

"And not let it get the best of us. Because after listening to the Admiral and all he accomplished, I'm not about to give up now."

"Me neither," said Jennifer. "But maybe we should do something that takes our mind off it for a while. We won't give up, but a break from work might do us some good."

"Why don't we take that long weekend and go camping like we've been talking about?"

"We've sure talked about it enough. Why don't we just do it?"

"How about next weekend?" asked Albert.

"I don't know if I'll be finished with that proposal I'm working ... oops! That sounds like trading results for excuses. I'll make sure I'm finished by Thursday afternoon, no matter what, and we can take Friday off and come back Sunday evening. What do you think?"

Winning Habits

"Let's do it. We can just go to Cuyamaca so we won't spend all weekend driving. It'll be great to get out into the woods again."

Jennifer dove into her project to make sure it would be finished on time.

Thursday evening while Jennifer was finishing up late at work, Albert bought all the groceries and supplies they'd need and loaded the car.

Friday morning they woke up at the crack of dawn, loaded Digger into the back seat, and took off. They were the first to arrive at the campground, which allowed them to have first pick of campsites. They chose a secluded area way in the back so they could get as much peace and quiet as possible.

"This is the first time we've ever been 'first on' at a campground," said Jennifer.

"I know, and look at the neat spot we got," replied Albert. "Maybe 'first on, last off' pays dividends away from work."

"Think about it. What we do as a family or for pleasure is every bit as important as what we do at work. So if we apply the habits at work, why shouldn't we apply them to everything else we do?"

"We should. Actually, we did already and look how it paid off."

They settled in to the campsite and went exploring.

Winning Habits

The weather was perfect and it turned out to be a glorious day. Digger enjoyed himself and made the trip all that more enjoyable for Jennifer and Albert. That night they cooked over the campfire and then roasted some-mores and reminisced as they tried to name the different constellations they could see in the star-filled sky.

The next day they decided to follow a nearby trail that led to a huge rock formation they wanted to explore.

After a brisk, forty-five minute hike, they reached the rock formation. Some of the huge boulders in the formation were bigger than most houses.

Digger immediately began nosing around the base as Jennifer and Albert walked around the side to find a place to climb up into the formation.

Jennifer found a three-sided chimney that extended just above her head and enthusiastically began to work her way up. She was able to push against either side to gain enough leverage to reach her arm up over the top.

She struggled to gain a handhold on top of the ledge. Unbeknown to Jennifer, the place where she was grasping around for a handhold was only inches from the den of a forty-inch-long red diamond rattlesnake!

The clawing motion of Jennifer's hand awakened the snake. Without hesitation, it struck! The deadly

serpent drove both fangs into the back of her hand, injecting its potentially lethal poison behind the pad of her palm.

Jennifer screamed and pushed back out of the chimney, falling onto the ground with the snake's fangs still imbedded in her hand.

Albert and Digger came running.

Without hesitation, Albert grabbed the snake just in front of its rattles and yanked it free. Instinctively he slung it like a whip, smashing the snake's head against the side of the rock. He then flung the writhing carcass into a nearby bush and rushed to Jennifer's aid.

"It stings," she said. She was now sitting up next to the rock with her good hand wrapped around the wrist of her injured hand. The fang marks were more oval than round because of the way Albert had jerked the snake away.

A little blood and a few drops of yellowish liquid oozed from the wounds.

"Let it bleed if you can," said Albert. "It looks like that's getting some of the poison out."

"It really stings. How are we going to get help?"

Albert reached into his fanny pack and pulled out a snake bite kit. He quickly opened it and took out the suction cup.

Winning Habits

"Here. Prop yourself against the rock. Use this suction cup to get as much out of those two holes as you can. I'll see if my cell phone works here."

She started pumping the suction cup as quickly as possible while Albert pulled his cell phone from his fanny pack and dialed 911.

"Highway patrol emergency," the dispatcher answered.

Albert explained the situation.

"I'm going to put you on hold for a minute while I contact some other agencies we need to get involved. Don't go away," directed the dispatcher.

"I'll be here," said Albert. Then to Jennifer: "How are you doing?"

"It still really stings, but I'm getting some stuff out of there."

"How about the rest of you?"

"Okay, I guess," she said.

Albert retrieved a bottle of water from his fanny pack. "Here, have a drink of water."

Jennifer took a swig. Then Albert splashed some water on the wounds to wash them clean and make it easier for her to continue to apply suction.

Winning Habits

"Okay, I'm back now," the dispatcher's voice crackled in the cell phone.

"Still here," replied Albert.

"Good. We don't want her walking out. An hour's walk is too far. That amount of activity would just speed up the circulation of the poison through her system. The park rangers say there's a clearing a few hundred yards farther up the trail that's big enough for a chopper. Life Flight will be taking off in about three or four minutes, but finding you and the clearing may be a problem. Park Rangers are coming in from the trailhead, but they won't get there until after Life Flight arrives."

"How about if I go to the clearing and wave them in?" asked Albert.

"That's what we want you to do. And stay connected with me so we can relay any messages."

"You got it," replied Albert.

"And by the way," said the dispatcher, "how's your cell phone battery?"

"Fully charged," responded Albert. "Shouldn't be a problem."

Albert encouraged Jennifer to take another drink from the bottle of water, and then he set it beside her. Beads of sweat had broken out on her upper lip. She appeared flush. He left Digger by her side and took off up the trail.

Winning Habits

He reached the clearing just as he heard the sound of the helicopter's engine gaining strength through the trees.

"I'm at the clearing and I can hear the helicopter, but I can't see it," Albert informed the dispatcher.

"Does it sound like it's getting closer?"

"It's definitely headed my way. I just can't see it yet. I'm going to the middle of the clearing."

At that instant the helicopter whooshed in over the treetops and passed above the clearing in a noisily spectacular fly-over. Albert waved with both arms and jumped up and down as the pilot waved back and circled around to land.

Albert retreated to the edge of the clearing as the pilot gently set the helicopter down in the center of the grassy meadow.

As soon as the chopper landed, a doctor and an assistant sprang out and dashed—stooping to avoid the still-rotating rotors—toward Albert. The doctor carried a medical pack and the assistant carried a lightweight stretcher made from aluminum and canvas.

"They're here and on the ground!" Albert shouted to the dispatcher over the sound of the chopper. "We're going to get Jennifer."

Without saying anything, Albert waved to the two to follow him. The three scurried down the trail toward Jennifer.

Winning Habits

When they arrived, Albert noticed that she looked much worse. Her skin looked pale and clammy, and she looked tired, almost groggy. The doctor immediately knelt by her side and began inspecting the bite.

"Hi, I'm Doctor Goodbody. Looks like you've done a good job of trying to get some of that bad stuff out of there."

"Thanks," said Jennifer.

"Once we get some antivenin in you, this should clear up pretty quick. But we're not going to do that until we get you back to the ER. For now, we're just going to start an IV and get you to the hospital where we can have more control over everything. It's a good thing that you had that little suction cup to start getting the poison out of there as soon as possible. The less that's in there, the fewer potential problems we're likely to encounter."

He swabbed the inside of her elbow and inserted an IV to which he connected a saline bottle.

"Now let's just get you on this stretcher and to the helicopter. If you can keep that suction cup working all the way in, it would help a great deal."

Jennifer scooted over and lay down on the stretcher and renewed her efforts with the suction cup.

Albert and the assistant carried the stretcher while the doctor walked alongside holding the IV bag. In a few minutes they arrived at the helicopter, whose engines were shut down. They quickly loaded Jennifer in and secured her and the stretcher. The pilot started up the engines even before they had finished securing her, and in no time the helicopter was headed to the emergency room with its precious cargo.

However, there wasn't room in the helicopter for Albert and Digger, so they were left behind. Albert immediately phoned Mrs. O'Reilly. She was grateful for the call. She immediately called the Admiral and both went to meet Jennifer at the hospital.

Albert and Digger blazed back down the trail at record-breaking speed. By the time Albert had broken camp and loaded everything into the car, Mrs. O'Reilly and the Admiral had arrived at the hospital and Albert was able to get a cell phone update. Jennifer had been given the antivenin and a dose of pain reliever, and she was resting comfortably.

Albert drove back home, dropped Digger off, and headed to the hospital, arriving about noon.

Shortly after Albert arrived, the doctor popped into Jennifer's emergency room cubicle to give an update.

"Look's like everything's going by the book, so we should be letting you out of here in about an hour or so. We just want to keep you here a little longer to make sure there are no delayed side effects from the antivenin. This turned out to be a relatively easy case to treat because you started early with the suction cup."

"I've wondered about that," said Jennifer. "I didn't know you kept a snake bite kit in your fanny pack, Albert."

"I didn't until recently. But there was an article in last Sunday's paper about this being the time of year snakes begin to get active, and I was thinking about our trip and how important it can be to solve problems in advance, so when I went shopping for supplies I picked one up. That's when I decided to put my cell phone in the fanny pack as well. Having that phone was helpful, too."

"Those were lifesaving decisions, Albert," said Mrs. O'Reilly.

"Sure were," said the doctor. "People die from these bites. And this one looks like it was from a pretty healthy snake that got its fangs in deep, so it probably unloaded a good dose of poison. Getting some of it out quickly was a big factor in being able to treat it effectively. And of course, getting Life Flight to her quickly also made a huge difference."

"Admiral, it looks like the secrets you shared with us are going to become a permanent part of our personal lives every bit as much as our work lives," said Jennifer.

"Before this weekend, we were becoming a bit disillusioned," added Albert. "But if anything has taught us to be persistent in applying these habits, this experience is it."

Winning Habits

The Admiral and Mrs. O'Reilly beamed with pride.

And so they persisted. They stayed focused and supported each other, both in building their careers and in strengthening their relationship.

In fact, they were so focused that they gave little thought to whether or not anyone else had noticed anything at all about the changes they made in their habits. After a few months Albert and Jennifer stopped noticing them as well. The reason they stopped noticing them was because the new habits had become a natural part of them—they truly became habits because both of them practiced the new behaviors consistently and without conscious effort in everything they did. The habits benefited them in every aspect of their lives.

Then a year later Albert received two offers for promotion in one month!

The first one surprised him because he had been so immersed in his work that he hadn't even given any thought to his personal advancement. Besides, it was in another department in which he had never even considered working.

Another department! I wonder how they heard about me, he thought. *Everybody knows! The Admiral was right. Sooner or later, everybody does know.*

Winning Habits

After discussing the offer with Jennifer, he turned it down. Even though it would have meant a nice pay increase, it was in an area that didn't inspire Albert. They were afraid that if he took it and couldn't be enthusiastic, it might ultimately lead to a setback in the long run.

But the next offer came not much later, almost on top of the first.

It was a real opportunity for Albert in the direction he wanted to take his career. Without much discussion they agreed it was obviously a great move, so he jumped on it.

The following weekend they took the Admiral and Mrs. O'Reilly to the nicest restaurant in San Diego to celebrate—the first of many such celebrations Jennifer and Albert would share in what promised to be a long, fulfilling life together.

The End